# The War of 1812 on the Genesee River

## A Documentary Journey

Christopher Pieczynski

ISBN: 978-0-557-32483-5

© 2010 Christopher Pieczynski

# Contents

Introduction     3

<u>Notes on the Visits of American and British Naval Vessels to the Genesee River, 1809-1814</u>, by Franklin Hanford     6

The War of 1812 on the Genesee River: A Documentary Journey     42

A Short Biography of Franklin Hanford

Illustrations     68

Bibliography     70

# Introduction

The upcoming bicentennial of the War of 1812 will no doubt focus on the enduring legacies of that war: the burning of Washington, the Star Spangled Banner, the sea battles of the USS *Constitution*, and the Battle of New Orleans. While these occurrences are significant, and provide some of the key turning points in the war that ultimately shaped this country, they are but a few of the many battles, skirmishes, and incidents of the war. Unfortunately, many of these other events will not be recognized for their significance. The incidents along the Genesee River in New York are just some of the examples of the oft neglected minor theaters of the war. It is easy to understand why. The area along the Genesee River, both upriver around the modern city of Rochester and along the shores of Lake Ontario, never saw a battle, never had any significant military presence, and at best held only a minor level of strategic value. Despite these facts, the few inhabitants of this area faced constant threat of British plunder or invasion and had almost continuous "visits" from both American and British forces during the extent of the war.

Sixty miles to the west of the Genesee River lies Fort Niagara at the junction of the Niagara River and Lake Ontario. Like the Niagara, the Genesee River flows north, passes over a rather significant escarpment creating a cascade only about half the height of the one at Niagara, and empties into Lake Ontario.[1] About sixty miles to the east lies Oswego and the location of Fort Ontario. The Genesee River, a convenient midpoint between these two critical military posts, proved its value during the war as a supply center, safe harbor, and embarkation and debarkation point for forces heading east or west into battle. Little of its military value was widely known though as the region generally receives only a footnote at best in popular accounts. Individual memoirs from the local citizens and area histories often mention incidents in the war but there was never a complete accounting of the activities in the area. For almost a century after the war ended, these piecemeal accounts were the extent of the what was known about the

---

[1] The Genesee River actually has three waterfalls and several sections of rapids over its 157 mile length. The fall at Rochester is the tallest at 80 feet.

War of 1812 along the Genesee River until a retired Admiral by the name of Franklin Hanford brought the war history of the region to life.

It was over a quarter of a century ago that I stumbled upon Franklin Hanford's <u>Notes on the Visits of American and British Naval Vessels to the Genesee River</u> while browsing the card catalog at the Buffalo and Erie County Public Library. Not one of the popular works on the War of 1812, it was relegated to the storage stacks in the library basement. Once this 1911 vintage item was retrieved from its subterranean home, I found that this 16 page long essay was number 66 of 300 copies, printed for private distribution, signed by the author, with no sign of ever being checked out of the library!

Although an obscure work, Hanford provides an exciting account of the naval activity, both British and American, in or around the Genesee River during the War of 1812. Using first-hand accounts from the soldiers, sailors, and citizens involved in the actions in the Genesee River area, Hanford paints a vivid picture of frontier life and defense against an enemy determined to threaten the remote settlements in the area. This excellent work may have very well been lost if it was not reprinted by the Rochester Historical Society in the 1924 edition of <u>Rochester Historical Society Publications</u>. Even so, it remains an obscure work, not even listed most bibliographies of the War of 1812.

Hanford's well written, and sometimes amusing account is provided here in its entirety. Although fairly comprehensive, one can only wonder if there was more to the story to the naval activities near the Genesee. Two works, both published in Rochester History, deserve note. The first is "War on Lake Ontario: 1812-1815" by Ruth Marsh and Dorothy S. Truesdale.[2] Marsh and Truesdale cover many of the same incidents as Hanford and even use Hanford's work as a source for many of the eyewitness testimony. The other work is "The Genesee River During the War of 1812" by Lillian Roemer.[3] Roemer use more archival materials to highlight the activities along the Genesee area and makes an excellent case that the raids at Charlotte, Sodus, and Pultneyville were the result of inadequate British provision. Much of the pre-war trade with Canada around Lake Ontario originated in the Genesee area. Again, Hanford is used to provide many of the first-hand accounts.

A further search of documentary collections and archives turns up additional material, not contained in Hanford's or the subsequent

---

[2] See <u>Rochester History</u>, vol. IV, October, 1942, no. 4.

[3] See <u>Rochester History</u>, vol. LIII, Fall, 1991, No. 4.

works on the area, that indeed makes the Genesee River area a hotbed of military activity during the War of 1812. This additional documentation contains sources that would not necessarily have been available to Hanford during the course of his research. As with most historical research, new sources are found almost as soon as the "definitive" account of an event is published. This study is designed to complement, and not supersede, Hanford's excellent work. As we approach the bicentennial of the War of 1812, this documentary journey will hopefully give a more comprehensive picture of the naval activities near the Genesee.

# Notes on the Visits of American and British Naval Vessels To the Genesee River 1809-1814

## By Franklin Hanford

It is difficult for the summer residents who people the shores of Lake Ontario from Nine Mile Point on the east to Manitou Beach on the west of the Genesee river, or for the holiday makers who wander among the trivial or amusing shows of Ontario Beach park at Charlotte to realize that the now peaceful waters of "the beautiful lake," as the Iroquois called it, were once plowed by hostile fleets. And yet, for a period of three years, nearly a century ago, during our war of 1812-14 with Great Britain, both American and British fleets appeared off the Genesee at intervals, and the pioneers of Monroe county witnessed naval maneuvers, heard the sound of an enemy's guns, and actually gathered to resist the invasion of their country.

It is proposed to mention here all the authenticated visits of American and British naval vessels to the mouth of the Genesee river up to the year 1815. While it is generally supposed that no men-of-war's men ever entered the Genesee in a government craft before the year 1812, there was certainly one such visit as early as June, 1089, nearly three years before the commencement of the War of 1812. An entertaining account of the visit will be found in J. Fenimore Cooper's "Lives of Distinguished American Naval Officers," published in 1846, in two volumes. In the second volume Cooper devotes thirty-

Melancthon Taylor Woolsey

three pages to his friend, Melancthon Taylor Woolsey, U.S. Navy. Following Cooper's account it appears that in 1808, our relations with Great Britain being strained, Woolsey, who was then a lieutenant, was selected by the Navy department to proceed to Oswego and superintend the construction of a brig of sixteen guns for service on Lake Ontario, and to command the first regular armament ever made under the Union on our inland waters. Woolsey took with him to Oswego two midshipmen, Messrs. Gamble and Cooper, the latter being James Cooper (whose name was afterwards changed to James Fenimore Cooper), the celebrated American novelist and naval historian. They spent the winter at Oswego and in the spring of 1809, the brig, named the Oneida, was launched and equipped for service. Her contractors were Christian Bergh and Henry Eckford, both of whom became eminent naval constructors.

Woolsey now decided to take a holiday and get a view of Niagara. Manning and provisioning the Oneida's launch he and Midshipman Cooper sailed from Oswego late in June, 1809. Relying upon the boat's sails, only four seamen from the Oneida's crew were taken along, and as they soon met strong head winds, there was not enough force to do much with the oars. Three times they beat up to a headland called the Devil's Nose [which is in the present town of Hamlin, Monroe county] before they could pass it. "Four nights were passed in the boat, two on the beach, and one in a hut on the banks of the Genesee, a few miles below the falls, and of course quite near the present site of Rochester." Their provisions having failed they were actually suffering for food. One old seaman of the crew, who had passed forty years on the lake, and knew the position of every one of the few dwellings near the shore between Oswego and Niagara, guided the two officers to some log huts where they obtained a loaf of bread, two pies, and a gallon of milk. Returning to the launch, sail was made and the

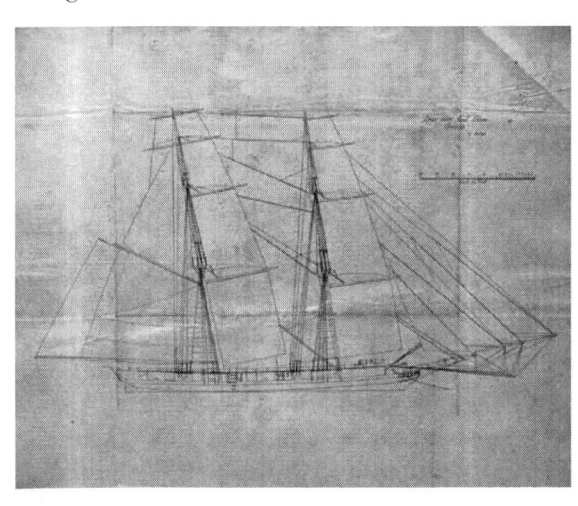

Plan of the *Oneida*

party proceeded, but "hunger and head winds again brought the adventurers to a stand. A solitary hut was known to be at no great distance inland from the point where the boat now was, and again the party landed," having been driven to leeward of the river. "The boat entered by a narrow inlet into a large bay that was familiarly called Gerundegutt (Irondequoit), and was hauled up for the night. The whole party bivouacked supperless." Next morning, however, they found a house, a mile or two inland, and bought a sheep for a half eagle. Woolsey contrived to make a sort of soup of part of the mutton. Having appeased their hunger, they again set out for the westward, but again the weather was foul and squally. In crossing Genesee bay, the boat nearly filled and the had to bear up again for the river. "Here the party passed another night, in a solitary log cabin, at, or near a point where the steamers and other craft must now make their harbor. A little bread was got in exchange for some sheep, and milk was purchased." In the morning, however, they again headed to the west and finally got past the Devil's Nose and into the Niagara river. "It was the Fourth of July, [1809] and the launch entered the river with an American ensign set. It proceeded to Newark, where the two officers took up their quarters for a week. In an hour a deputation from Fort Niagara came across to inquire who had brought the American ensign, for the first time, in a man-of-war's boat, into that river. On being told, a formal invitation was given to join the other officers on the other side in celebrating the day."

"Woolsey and his party remained some time in and about Niagara. He passed up on the upper lake, and paid a visit on board the Adams, a brig that belonged to the War department. The return to Oswego was less difficult, and was accomplished in two days. These were the first movements by American man-of-war's men that ever occurred on the great lakes—waters that have since become famous by the deeds of McDonough, Perry, and Chauncey."

Woolsey remained on the Lake Ontario station until the close of the War of 1812, but Cooper not long after the trip to Niagara returned to the Atlantic coast. His winter at Oswego and his trip to Niagara by way of "Gerundegutt," the Genesee river, and the Devil's Nose gave him a personal knowledge of the inland sea and of the wilderness which then surrounded it, and to that experience we owe the vivid pictures of Lake Ontario drawn in his story of "The Pathfinder."

At the beginning of our second war with Great Britain, neither party to the contest had more than an insignificant force on Lake Ontario. The British had the greater number of vessels, but they lacked regular and experienced officers to command. Hence the American navy under Lieutenant Melancthon T. Woolsey, of our regular service, was able to hold in check the British squadron under the Canadian Commodore Earle during 1812, until the arrival of Captain Issac Chauncey, U.S. Navy, in October of that year, when he assumed command of our forces on the lake and continued in command during the rest of the war.

In May, 1813, Captain Sir James Lucas Yeo, of the Royal Navy, together with four captains, eight lieutenants, twenty-four midshipmen, and about 450 picked seamen, arrived on the scene of action, sent out by the home government especially for service on the lakes, and Sir James continued in command of the British forces there until the close of the war.

Both Chauncey and Yeo held the actual rank of captain, but by custom and courtesy were called commodore from the fact that they had command of squadrons.

The headquarters of the Americans was at Sacketts Harbor, and of the British, at Kingston. Both parties, from the beginning, made strenuous efforts to increase their fleets, especially by building vessels at the ports mentioned. The Americans, in 1812, purchased a number of small vessels and converted them into gunboats. Shipwrights and other mechanics were brought from the seaboard by both the British and American and employed constantly at shipbuilding until the war closed, by which time both fleets had some vessels of considerable size, mounting guns ranging from 6-pounders to 68-pounders.

**Commodore Chauncey**

Among the vessels sold to our government were several which were engaged in the lake commerce to and from the Genesee river. The following extract from the "Recollections of George C. Latta" in "Early Rochester Records," as published in the Rochester "Post Express" of May 27, 1911, refers to some of these vessels: "As early as 1809 Roswell Lewis & Co. of Ogdensburg built a schooner called the Experiment, Captain Holms, and began the forwarding business from Genesee to Ogdensburg. They afterwards built a vessel called the Captain Dickson and the schooner called the Genesee Packet, Captain Ober Meeyer. These vessels continued to do business between Ogdensburg and

Genesee river until the spring of 1812, when war was declared between the United States and Great Britain, and the vessels were then sold to the government and sent into service on the lake."

None of the American or British histories of naval operations on Lake Ontario which I have consulted, make any reference to events at or near the Genesee during the year 1812, though vessels of both nations were cruising on the lake during the latter part of that year, and there is good reason to believe that vessels of our squadrons ascended the river as high as Hanford's Landing, not only in 1812, but subsequently, for refuge, for recruits or for supplies. But I am able to quote from a broadside printed in 1843, which contains an address given by Mr. Donald McKenzie before the Mumford, N.Y. Lyceum in that year. Mr McKenzie was one of the Scotch pioneers who had settled near the Caledonia "Big Springs." He Said:

> In the latter part of the year 1812, being on a visit with my wife at her father's at the mouth of the river, he accompanied us on horseback to the residence of my brother-in-law, Abel Rowe, on the Ridge Road. The next morning, as we were mounting our horses to return, a messenger arrived witrh an express, stating that a British fleet was approaching the mouth of the river, and requesting Captain Rowe to call out the militia immediately. Returning, on our way towards the landing, we could hear distinctly the report of every cannon fired by the enemy. After leaving my wife with the family of my worthy friend, Benj. Fowle, at the landing, we hurried on as fast as possible to the mouth of the river. But nothing was to be seen of the fleet nor of the few families there. We rode immediately to my father-in-law's old log house, standing then on the very spot where now stands a United States Light House, fastened our horses, and from there, with my brother-in-law, William Hencher, jr., went on foot to the beach of the lake. We soon discovered the fleet sailing towards us, from the direction of Braddock's Bay, but not anticipating any danger, we remained on the spot until it approached quite near us. We were shortly saluted with a 24-pounder, which whistled through the bushes near where we stood, and entered the bank of the lake in our rear. This shot was in rather too close proximity to us to be agreeable. I afterwards dug the ball out of the bank and used it for a number of years to grind indigo with in my woolen factory.

The British squadron then, according to Mr. McKenzie, retreated "without landing or doing any injury." It was probably in command of Commodore Earle, a Canadian officer, and composed of the Royal George, and a brig, and two or three smaller vessels. Mr. McKenzie's visit was probably in October or November, 1812, as navigation closed by the middle of the latter month. I have endeavored to find out what became of the British shot, but regret to say that all traces of it is lost, as I learned from Mr. McKenzie's daughter, Miss Elizabeth McKenzie, and his nephew, Mr. William S. McKenzie, of Caledonia.

James Fenimore Cooper, in his History of the Navy of the United States, says that on June 16, 1813, Sir James Yeo went off the Genesee with his squadron where some provisions

were seized and carried away. The following official report from Commodore Yeo to Mr. John Wilson Croker, Secretary of the Admiralty, includes a reference to the event. It is given in "A Full and Correct Account of the Chief Naval Occurrences of the Late War between Great Britain and the United States of America," by William James, published at London, in 1817:

H.M.S. Wolf, Kingston, Upper Canada, 29th June, 1813.

Sir:

I have the honor to inform you, for the information of the Lords Commissioners of the Admiralty, that on the 3d instant, I sailed with His Majesty's squadron under my command from this port, to co-operate with our army at the head of the lake, and annoy the enemy by intercepting all supplies going to the enemy and thereby oblige his squadron to come out for its protection.

At daylight on the 8th, the enemy's camp was discovered close to us at Forty-mile creek. It being calm, the large vessels could not get in, but the Beresford, Captain Spilsbury, the Sir Sidney Smith, Lieutenant Majoribanks, and the gunboats under the orders of Lieutenant Anthony (first of this ship) succeeded in getting close under the enemy's batteries, and by a sharp and well-directed fire, soon obliged him to make a precipitate retreat, leaving all his camp equipage, provisions, stores, etc., behind, which fell into our hands. The Beresford also captured all his bateaux, laden with stores, etc. Our tropps immediately occupied the post. I then proceeded along to the westward of the enemy's camp, leaviong our army in front. On the 13th we captured two enemy schooners and some boats, going to the enemy with supplies; by them I received information that there was a depot of provisions at Genesee river. I accordingly proceeded off that river, landed some seamen and marines of the squadron, and brought off all the provisions found in the government stores; as also a sloop laden with grain for the army. On the 19th I anchored off the Great Sodas, landed a part of the 1st Regiment Royal Scots and took off 600 barrels of flour and pork, which had arrived there for their army.

I have the honor to be, etc.,

J.L. Yeo, Commodore.

Nearly all the writers on events connected with the local history of Monroe county and Western New York refer to this incident of the carrying away of provisions by Sir James Yeo's fleet. A very clear account of the affair is given by a writer in the Rochester "Post Express" of May 13, 1894, as follows:

Coming to anchor he sent a party ashore for plunder. There was no military organization at the mouth of the river and no opposition was offered. The enemy remained over night, keeping sentries posted, and retired to their ships next morning, taking salt, whisky, and provisions from the storehouse of Frederick Bushnell. George Latta, who was Bushnell's clerk at the time, obtained a receipt from the British officer for these goods. It has been said that the British hurriedly boarded their ships because they heard that an armed force was collecting at Hanford's Landing and intended to move against them. Probably the British remained until they had gathered the supplies they needed and left at their own convenience and in accordance with their original plan. At this time, the British squadron consisted of the Wolfe, Royal George, Moira, Melville, Beresford, Sidney Smith, and one or two gunboats.

"The Post Express" writer's view of the affair (that Commodore Yeo left at his own convenience and to carry out his original plan), is borne out by the British officer's letter quoted above. And it will be noted that while off the Genesee, on this occasion, he had on board the vessels of his fleet at least part of the First regiment of Royal Scots. It is not probable, therefore, that he was driven off by fear of the force of hurriedly gathered militia up the river.

Turner, in his History of the Phelps and Gorham's Purchase, says, with reference to the affair of June 16, 1813, that "the only restraint that was put upon a few captured citizens, was the preventing their going out to warn the inhabitants of the neighborhood of their presence," and that a body of armed men that had collected at Hanford's Landing "marched down, arriving at the Charlotte Landing just as the invaders were embarking on board their boats. Some shots were fired upon them, but from too great a distance to be made effective."

**Old Hanford Tavern as seen in 1883**

The men to whom Turner refers were probably those under the command of Lieutenant-Colonel Caleb Hopkins. The following letter to Hopkins from Major-General Amos Hall, of Ontario county, refers to the event under discussion:

> Bloomfield, June 16th, 1813
>
> 4 o'clock, P.M.
>
> Lt. Col. Caleb Hopkins,
>
> Sir: I this moment received your letter by Major Norton advising me of the landing of the enemy from their fleet off the mouth of the Genesee river. Your calling out your Regiment was perfectly correct. You will please to collect as many men as appearances will justify until the enemy's vessels leave the mouth of the river. It cannot be expected they will make much stay. But you will be able to judge of their movements by to-morrow morning. I shall expect you

will give me immediate notice if you think more force will be wanted.

Yours respectfully,

A. Hall

Hopkins at the time held the double position of collector of customs and inspector of customs at the port of Genesee, both commissions having been issued by President Madison, but his civic duties did not prevent his engaging in military pursuits, as is shown by the above letter.

The effect of this invasion was to spread alarm through the community and it was feared that the British Commodore might at some subsequent day land a large force of troops from his fleet and march up the river. Some families of settlers at and below the falls of the Genesee removed to other places. In several instances the women and children were sent away while the men of the family remained. The settlement and development of the Genesee region were much retarded by the War of 1812.

About August 10-12, 1813, according to Fenimore Cooper's account of Naval Operations on Lake Ontario, Commodore Chauncey, after a running fight with the British squadron at the western end of the lake, determined to run with his vessels for the Genesee, on account of a gale which had sprung up, but as the gale increased and two of his vessels had but a day's provisions on board, he stood in for Sacketts' Harbor, where he arrived August 13, 1813. The following is taken from Chauncey's official report to the Secretary of the Navy, dated on board the U.S. ship General Pike, 13th August, 1813, at Sacketts Harbor:

> Sir: I arrived here this day . . .
>
> The gale increasing very much, and as I could not go into Niagara with this ship, I determined to run to Genesee Bay, as a shelter for the small vessels, and with the expectation of being able to obtain provisions for the squadron, as we were nearly out, the Madison and Oneida having not a single day's on board when we arrived opposite Genesee Bay. I found there was every prospect of the gale's continuing, and if I did, I could run to this place, and provision the whole squadron with more certainty, and in nearly the same time that I could at Genesee, admitting that I could obtain provisions at that place.

After provisioning his ships for five weeks, Chauncey, according to Cooper, "sailed on another cruise the very day of his arrival. On the

16th, the squadron was off the Niagara, and the same day the enemy was made, being eight sail in all. Some maneuvering to obtain the wind followed, but it coming on to blow, the vessels ran into the mouth of the Genesee and anchored. The wind, however, freshened so much as to compel the whole squadron to weigh and bear up, forcing them down to the lake under easy canvas." The American squadron on this occasion consisted of the Pike, Madison, Oneida, Tompkins, Conquest, Ontario, Pert, and Lady of the Lake. As the gale continued to increase, Chauncey took his vessels to Sacketts' Harbor where they arrived on the 19th of August, 1813.

**Drawing of the engagement on August 10, 1813**

Following Cooper's History it appears that "on the 11th of September, [this was the day after Perry's victory on Lake Erie, September 10, 1813,] the enemy was becalmed off the Genesee, when the American vessels got a breeze and ran within gunshot, before the English squadron took the wind. A running fight, that lasted more than three hours, was the result; but the enemy escaped in consequence of his better sailing, it being out of the power of the American commander to close with more than two of his vessels, the Sylph being totally unfitted for that kind of combat. As the Pike succeeded in getting several broadsides at the enemy, he did not escape without being a good deal cut up, having, according to his own report, an officer and ten men

15

killed and wounded. The Pike was hulled a few times, and other trifling injuries were received, though no person was hurt. Previously to this affair, Commodore Chauncey had been joined by the Fair American and Asp. On the 12th, Sir James Yeo ran into Amherst bay, where the Americans were unable to follow him, on account of their ignorance of the shoals. It was supposed that the English commodore declined engaging on this occasion, in consequence of the smoothness of the water, it being policy to bring his enemy to action in blowing weather, when the American schooners would be nearly useless."

Nearly all writers on the history of the United States navy mention this skirmish off the Genesee. Willis J. Abbott in his "Blue Jackets of 1812," says: "On the 11th of September [1813] the enemies met near the mouth of the Genesee river and exchanged broadsides. A few of the British vessels were hulled, and, without more ado, hauled off into the shallow waters of Ambert [Amherst?] bay where the Americans could not follow them."

In John R. Spear's four-volume "History of the Navy," he says, referring to the operations on Lake Ontario in 1813:" On the day after Perry's victory, the two squadrons did have a brush at long range in a light breeze. It was a good day for the Yankee schooners and Sir James, by his own confession, sailed away after a few shots had been fired. The Americans lost nothing. The British lost four killed and seven wounded."

Theodore Roosevelt in his "Naval War of 1812," gives a very full discussion of the event. He says: "On the 11th of September a partial engagement, at very long range, in light weather, occurred near the mouth of the Genesee river; the Americans suffered no loss whatever, while the British had one midshipman and three seaman killed and seven wounded, and afterward ran into Amherst bay."

The latest American writer on the Naval War of 1812 is Captain Alfred T. Mahan, who, in his "Sea Power in its Relations to the War of 1812" says: "On one occasion, off the Genesee, on September 11, [1813] a westerly breeze carried the United States squadron within three-quarters of a kile of the enemy, before the latter felt it. A cannonade and pursuit of some hours followed, but without decisive results."

William James, the English author of "A Full and Correct Account of the Chief Naval Occurrences of the Late War between Great Britain and the U.S. of America," already referred to, says of this engagement off the Genesee: "The only shot received by the British fleet that wanted a plug, struck the Melville, and that so far under the water, the Captain Spilsbury had to run his guns in on one side, and out on the other, to enable him to stop it."

**Drawing of the engagement on Lake Ontario, September 11, 1813**

James also wrote "The Naval History of Great Britain," and in the London, 1837, edition of the six-volume work, he says: "On the 11th of September [1813], while the British squadron lay becalmed off the Genesee river the American fleet of eleven sail, by the aid of partial wind, succeeded in getting within range of their long 24- and 32-pounders, and during five hours cannonaded the British who did not fire a carronade, and had only six guns in all the squadron that could reach the enemy. At sunset a breeze sprang up from the westward when Sir James steered for the American fleet; but the American commodore avoided a close meeting and thus the affair ended. It was so far unfortunate for Sir James Yeo that he had a midshipman (William Ellery) and three seamen killed and seven wounded."

It will be seen that the English author's statement that Chauncy avoided a close contest is directly contrary to Sir James Yeo's own account of the affair which is given herewith in that officer's official report to Admiral Sir John Warren who was then in command of the British naval forces on the American coast. This report is taken from William Jame's "Naval Occurances," London, 1817:

H.M.s Ship Wolfe, off the False Duck Islands, on Lake Ontario, Sept. 12, 1813.
Sir:

I have the honor to acquaint you that H.M.'s squadron under my command, being becalmed on Genesee river, on the 11th instant, the enemy's fleet of eleven sail, having a partial wind, succeeded in getting within range of their long 24- and 32-pounders; and from their having the wind of us, and the dull sailing of some of our squadron, I found it impossible to bring them to close action. We remained in this mortifying situation five hours, having only six guns in the squadron that would reach the enemy; (not a carronade being fired); at sunset a breeze sprang up from the westward, when I steered for the False Duck Islands, under which the enemy could not keep the weather-gauge, but be obliged to meet us on equal terms. This, however, he carefully avoided.

**Sir James Yeo**

Although I have to regret the loss of Mr William Ellery, midshipman, and three seaman killed, I cannot but conceive it fortunate that none of the squadron have received material damage, which must have been considerable, had the enemy acted with the least spirit, and taken advantage of the superiority of position they possessed.

Inclosed is a list of killed and wounded.

Killed, 3; wounded, 7.

J.L. Yeo

In order to complete the account of this skirmish off the Genesee, Commodoore Chauncey's official report to the Secretary of the Navy is also given. It is taken from H.A. Fay's "Collection of the Official Accounts, in Detail, of all the Battles fought by Sea and Land, between the United States, and the Navy and Army of Great Britain, During the years 1812, 13, 14, & 15," published at New York, 1817:

On board the U.S.S. Gen. Pike off Duck Island, Sept. 13,1813.

Sir—

On the 7th, at daylight, the enemy's fleet was discovered close in with the Niagara river, wind from the southward. Made the signal, weighed with the fleet, (prepared for action) and stood out of the river, after him. He immediately made all sail to the northward; we made sail in chase, with our heavy schooners in tow-and have continued the chase, all round the lake, night and day, until yesterday morning, when he succeeded in getting into Amherst Bay, which is so little known to our pilots and said to be so full of shoals, that they are not willing to take me in there. I shall, however, (unless driven from my station by a gale of wind), endeavor to watch him so close, as to prevent his getting out upon the lake. During our long chase, we frequently got within from one to two miles of the enemy; but our heavy-sailing schooners prevented our closing in with him, until the 11th off Genesee river; we carried a breeze with us, while he lay becalmed, to within about three-fourths of a mile of him, when he took the breeze, and we had a running flight of three and a half hours; but by his superior sailing, he escaped me, and run into Amherst Bay, yesterday morning. In the course of our chase, on the 11th, I got several broadsides, from this ship, upon the enemy, which must have done him considerable injury, as many of the shot were seen to strike him, and people were observed, over the side, plugging shot-holes; a few shot struck our hull, and a little rigging was cut, but nothing of importance—not a man was hurt.

I was much disappointed, that Sir James refused to fight me, as he was so much superior in point of force, both in guns and men—having upwards of 20 guns more than we have, and throws a greater weight of shot.

This ship, the Madison, and Sylph, have each a schr. Constantly in tow; yet the others cannot sail as fast as the enemy's squadron, which gives him decidedly the advantage, and puts it in his power to engage me when and how he chooses.

I have the honor, &c

Isaac Chauncey.

Hon. W. Jones, Sec'y Navy

Roosevelt condemns both Sir James Yeo and Commodore Chauncey for not making the most of the opportunity to fight on this occasion, and calls attention to the fact that each claimed that the other tried to avoid a battle. He says, "both sides admit that Yeo got the worst of it and ran away, and it is only a question as to whether Chauncey followed him or not."

Cooper, whose opinions on our naval operations are always worth consideration, thought the Chauncey behaved well and praises his conduct while in command of the naval forces on Lake Ontario; he also praises Yeo's ability and energy, but is of the opinion that Yeo had orders from higher authority to avoid a general contest for the supremacy of the lake, unless absolutely sure for a victory, and that this accounts for not being willing to bring on a real battle.

In this affair off the Genesee, the American had ten vessels as follows:

CHAUNCEY'S SQUADRON.

Ships.

Pike. Tonnage, 875; crew, 300; broadside metal, 360 lbs; armament, 28 long 24-pounders.

Madison. Tonnage, 593; crew, 200; broadside metal, 364 lbs; armament, 24 short 32s.

Brig.

Oneida. Tonnage, 243; crew, 100; broadside metal, 172 lbs; armament, 16 short 24s.

Drawing of schooner *Growler* captured by the British

Schooners.

Sylph. Tonnage, 300; crew, 70; broadside metal, 146 lbs; armament, 4 long 32-pounders, and 6 long 6s.

Conquest. Tonnage, 82; crew, 40; broadside metal, 56 lbs; armament, 1 long 32-pounder, 1 long 12-pounder and 4 long 6s.

Thompkins. Tonnage, 96; crew, 40; broadside metal, 62 lbs; armament, 1 long 32-pounder, 1 long 12-pounder and 6 long 6s.

Ontario. Tonnage, 53; crew, 35; broadside metal, 44 lbs; armament, 1 long 32-pounder and 1 long 12-pounder.

Fair American. Tonnage, 53; crew, 30; broadside metal, 36 lbs; armament, 1 long 24-pounder, 1 long 12-pounder.

Pert. Tonnage, 50; crew, 25; broadside metal, 24 lbs; armament, 1 long 24-pounder.

Asp. Tonnage, 57; crew, 25; broadside metal, 25 pounds; armament, 1 long 24-pounder.

Commodore Yeo's squadron was composed of six vessels as follows:

YEO'S SQUADRON.

Ships.

Wolfe. Tonnage, 637; crew, 220; broadside metal, 392 lbs; armament, 1 long 24-pounder, 8 long 18s, 4 short 68s and 10 short 32s.

Royal George. Tonnage, 510; crew, 200; broadside metal, 360 lbs; armament, 3 long 18s, 2 short 68s, and 16 short 32s.

Brigs.

Melville. Tonnage, 279; crew, 80; broadside metal, 172 lbs; armament, 2 long 18s and 12 short 32s.

Moira. Tonnage, 262; crew, 100; broadside metal, 153 lbs; armament, 2 long 9s and 12 short 24s.

Schooners.

Sydney Smith. Tonnage, 216; crew, 80; broadside metal, 172 lbs; armament, 2 long 12s and 10 short 32s.

Beresford. Tonnage, 187; crew, 70; broadside metal, 87 lbs; armament, 1 long 24-pounder, 1 long 9-pounder, and 6 short 18s.

The above tables are taken from Roosevelt's "Naval War of 1812" and were compiled by him after a careful study of the reports of both British and American authorities.

To recapitulate: Chauncey had ten vessels with a total tonnage of 2,402, 865 men in their crews, and 98 guns throwing a broadside of 1,288 lbs. of metal. And Yeo had six vessels with a total tonnage of 2,091, 770 men in their crews, and 92 guns throwing a broadside of 1,374 lbs. of metal.

Chauncey's squadron was the largest and he had the greater number of men and guns. Yeo's squadron was much more homogeneous and he had a slight advantage in the total weight of broadside. If the British commodore had really wanted to fight it would seem that this was an opportunity not to be missed.

Of the American vessels engaged in this affair, the Flagship Pike was commanded by Captain Arthur Sinclair; the Madison, by Master Commandant William M. Crane; the Oneida, by Lieutenant Thomas Brown; the Sylph, by Master Commandant Melancthon T. Woolsey; the Conquest by Lieutenant John Pettigrew; the Tompkins, by Lieutenant William Bolton Finch; the Pert, by Lieutenant Samuel W. Brown, and the Asp, by Lieutenant Smith. It is uncertain who commanded the Ontario and Fair American. Nor can the names of the commanding officers of the British ships be given at present with certainty, except that the Royal George was in command of Captain William Howe Mulcaster.

While the writers on naval affairs give considerable space to this 11th September, 1813, skirmish, few of the historians of Monroe county and Western New York give it space. But it will be of interest to quote from Turner's "Phelps and Gorham's Purchase" in order to get the point of view of onlookers from the shore. Turner's account is as follows:

> Toward the last of September, of the same year, [1813] both the British and American fleets were at the upper end of the lake, Commodore Chauncey making frequent demonstrations to Sir James Yeo, of his readiness to contend for the supremacy of the lake, but the latter declining, and gradually making his way down the lake. Arriving off the mouth of the Genesee river the fleet was becalmed and lay almost motionless upon the water. The inhabitants of Charlotte supposed the fleet had anchored preparatory to another landing, expresses were sent into the country; men armed and unarmed flocked from the back-woods settlements, and in a few hours a considerable number of men collected ready to fight or to run, as chances of invasion should make it expedient. While anxiously watching the British fleet, expecting every moment to see their boats coming toward the shore, a light breeze sprang up, and, soon

after, the fleet of Commodore Chauncey was seen rounding Bluff Point. It was a welcome advert, was hailed with joyous shouts from the shore; at a moment when a weak force had supposed themselves about to engage with a vastly superior one, succor had come--a champion had stepped, or rather sailed in, quite equal to the task of defence, in fact seeking the opportunity that seemed to have occurred. Commodore Chauncey brought his fleet within a mile from the shore, and when it was directly opposite the becalmed fleet of the enemy, he opened a tremendous fire upon it. At first a sheet of flame arose from the American fleet, and then a dense cloud of smoke that rolled off before a light breeze, blowing off shore, as completely shut out the British fleet from view as if the curtains of night had been suddenly drawn; while the American fleet remained in full view. The fire was returned, but as the breeze increased both moved down the lake, continuing the exchange shots until after dark. The fire upon the British fleet was pretty effective, until by it superior sailing abilities it had got out of the reach of Commodore Chauncey's guns. The British fleet was a good deal disabled; and an officer and ten men were either killed or wounded. A vessel of the American fleet got a few shots through its hull, but no one was either killed or wounded on board of it.

We find no further references to events at the mouth of the Genesee during 1813, except the following from Cooper and Roosevelt:

Cooper says that on the 13th of November, 1813, "Commodore Chauncey, who had now almost an undisturbed possession of the lake, went to the Genesee, where, on the 16th of the month, he took on board 1,100 men, belonging to the army of General Harrison. A severe gale came on, by which the vessels were separated, some being driven as far west as the head of the lake. The transports, into which most of the small schooners were now converted, having been finally dispatched, the commodore went off Kingston again to occupy the enemy and to cover the passage of the troops. All the transports had arrived on the 21st but the Julia, which did not get in until a few days later. The Fair American had gone ashore near the Niagara during the gale, but was got off, and reached the harbor [Sacketts harbor] on the 27th. By this time the navigation of the lake was virtually closed, and it being too late to attempt any naval operations, while the duty of transporting the troops and stores had been successfully performed, preparations were made to lay the vessels up for the winter.

23

Thus terminated the naval operations on Lake Ontario during the season of 1813."

Roosevelt's account of this duty of Chauncey's squadron is that after October, 1813, "Yeo remained in Kingston, blockaded by Chauncey for most of the time; on November 10th he came out and was at once chased back into port by Chauncey, leaving the latter for the rest of the season entirely undisturbed. Accordingly, Chauncey was able to convert his small schooners into transports. On the 17th these transports were used to convey 1,100 men of the army of General Harrison from the mouth of the Genesee to Sacketts Harbor, while Chauncey blockaded Yeo in Kingston. The duty of transporting troops and stores went on till the 27th, when everything had been accomplished; and a day or two afterward navigation closed."

The following extract from a letter from Hamlet Scranton to his father Abraham Scranton gives a good idea of the state of excitement which existed among the pioneers of Western New York in general and of Rochester in particular, at the close of the year 1813:

Rochester, Sunday Evening, 26th December, 1813.

Dear sir:

You will doubtless have news of the serious affair on our frontiers before you receive this. On Sunday morning the 19th, the British troops and Indians crossed the river at the five mile meadows; they proceeded to Fort Niagara, entered, and commenced the horrid massacre of the sick and wounded. . . . Our first accounts stated that all that came in their way were butchered without regard to age or sex, but it is not correct. But the distress of the inhabitants whose lot it was to fall into their hands is indescribable. Daily are passing here in sleighs and wagons, families deprived of their all. Not a cent of money, no provision, no bedding; children barefoot, etc., all depending on the charity of the people. The enemy continued their ravages from Sunday morning until Monday afternoon. . . . Early on Tuesday morning an express arrived in our village relative to the above affair; orders were issued by the captains of companies, the men were warned out forthwith and the next morning whole companies were on their march. . . . On Thursday morning an express arrived at the break of day, that the enemy were landing from their boats at Oak Orchard Creek about forty miles from this and were proceeding this way desolating the country and it was expected another party would be in at the mouth of the Genesee river. All were alarmed. Some thought it best to be on the move; other did not apprehend danger. The militia were all called upon to repair to the bridge and the mouth of the river; the whole country in confusion. Captain Stone (who keeps the tavern on the other side of the river) sent in all directions to assemble his company of dragoons (a very fine company), sent his children to Bloomfield, and made preparations to move his most valuable effects at short notice. The merchants went to packing goods (of which there are four very full stores here), some running balls, others making cartridges. I yoked my oxen, packed up all our bedding and clothing and moved my family up to the log house on a back road about a mile from the bridge on the east side of the river, together with all my provisions and cooking utensils that were of immediate use. Before night our village was crowded with militia coming in all night and next; but the whole of this proved to be a false alarm; the enemy have never been but ten miles this side of Lewiston. The next week I moved back again to the village, and now rest secure, I think, for this winter. Israel and his family and one other family remained in the village all night, the rest crossed the river.

Fear of further appearances of the British fleet induced the military authorities of the state to organize a force to prepare for a possible invasion.

This force was composed entirely of militia, and, in the spring of 1814, there was a company of about fifty men which had been recruited by Captain Isaac W. Stone, stationed either at Charlotte or at Rochester. Brigadier-General Peter B. Porter had command of all the militia in Western New York, and In April, 1814, he had sent to Captain Stone from Canandaigua two cannon, an eighteen-pounder and a four—pounder, the latter of brass, for the defense of the Genesee river. Elisha Ely, in his reminiscences of early days in Rochester, printed in 1848, in a pamphlet entitled "Proceedings at the Annual festivals of the Pioneers of Rochester, Held at Blossom Hall, September 30, 1847, and October 12, 1848," gives an amusing account of the arrival of these guns at Rochester. He says:

I think it was in April, 1814, an eighteen-pound cannon and a four-pounder, the latter of brass, were sent by General P.B. Porter to the care of Captain (afterwards Colonel) Isaac W. Stone. It required seventeen yoke of oxen to draw the eighteen-pounder through from Culvers to this place, such was the state of the roads. With the cannon came powder and ball. We soon collected some powder in the village and had a few rounds, very much to the amusement of all of us. It was suggested that we should see what effect a ball would have. The cannon was placed on Main Street at the corners near Blossom's hotel. On the rise of ground very near the residence of the lamented General Matthews, a large limb about forty feet from the ground was cut from a tree, which left a white spot for a target. I went rather clandestinely to Captain Stone's barn, got a ball and intended getting it into the cannon without his noticing it. He observed it, however, and said I ought not to waste the public property in that way. I replied "Never mind, Captain, we will find it again." "Find the devil," said he. Enos Stone and Frederick Hanford acted as chief engineers, and myself as assistant. All things being ready, the cannon was fired. The ball struck the tree about four feet below the mark. The top quivered a moment and fell. This was our experience in gunnery. The boys soon brought us the ball, so that the United States lost nothing by the operation.

The expected British fleet actually appeared off the Genesee on the evening of May 14, 1814, in command of Commodore Yeo, and came to anchor. Commodore Chauncey's squadron, at this time, had not left Sackett's Harbor, and, indeed, did not get away from that place until July 31$^{st}$, owing to delays in getting guns and stores for his new vessels, built during the preceeding winter. Hence Yeo had practically the entire command of the lake until after midsummer.

**Engagement between USS *General Pike* and HMS Wolfe**

From William James's "Naval History of Great Britain," Vol. VI., from Roosevelt's "Naval War of 1812," and from an article in the Rochester "Post Express" of May 19, 1894, the following table, giving the details as to Yeo's squadron in May, 1814, is compiled. In addition to the table, there were a number of smaller ones, gunboats, barges, etc.:

YEO'S SQUADRON.

Ships.

Prince Regent, flag ship, a new vessel, Captain Richard James Lawrence O'Connor; tonnage, 1,450; crew, 485; broadside metal, 872 pounds; armament, 32 long 24-pounders; 4 short 68s; 22 short 32s; total, 58 guns.

Princess Charlotte, a new vessel, Captain William Howe Mulcaster; tonnage, 1,215; crew, 315; broadside metal, 604 pounds; armament, 26 long 24s; 2 short 68s; 14 short 32s; total, 42 guns.

Montreal, former name Wolfe, Captain Stephen Popham; tonnage, 637; crew, 220; broadside metal, 258 pounds; armament, 7 long 24, 18 long 18s; total, 25 guns.

Niagara, former name Royal George, Captain Francis Brockell Splisbury; tonnage, 510; crew, 200; broadside metal, 332 pounds; armament, 2 long 12s, 20 short 32s; total, 22 guns.

Brigs.

Charwell, former name Moira, Captain Alexander Dobbs; tonnage, 279; crew, 110; broadside metal, 236 pounds; armament, 2 long 12s, 14 short 32s; total 16 guns.

Star, former name Melville, Captain Charles Anthony; tonnage, 262; crew, 110; broadside metal, 236 pounds; armament, 2 long 12s, 14 short 24s; total, 16 guns.

Netly, former name Beresford, Lieutenant Owens; tonnage, 216; crew, 100; broadside metal, 180 pounds; armament, 2 long 12s, 14 short 24s; total 16 guns.

Magnet, former name Sidney Smith, Captain Henry Collier; tonnage, 187; crew, 80; broadside metal, 156 pounds; armament, 2 long 12s, 12 short 24s; total 14 guns.

Summary.

Eight vessels; tonnage, 4,756; crews, 1,620; broadside metal, 2,874 pounds; guns, 209.

This was a powerful force compared with the 600 to 800 militia who could at the most be brought to oppose their landings had Commodore Yeo decided to take possession of the mouth of the Genesee river. But it is more than probable that, had Yeo attempted to send a force into the country and away from the range of the naval guns, the militia would have been able to prevent much progress towards Rochester.

None of the naval writers concerning events on Lake Ontario in 1814 mentions this appearance of Yeo's squadron off the Genesee; but all the writers on the history of Rochester, of Monroe county, or of Western New York give it considerable space, for while it was of little moment in considering the campaigns of the year, or in its effect on the general result, it was a very important event in our local history and created great excitement all throughout the Genesee Country, and from Canandaigua to Le Roy and Batavia. One of the earliest accounts of the affair is found in the first Rochester Directory, published at Rochester in 1827, and is as follows:

"On the 14th of May [1814] Sir James L. Yeo, admiral of the British fleet on Lake Ontario, anchored off the harbor at the mouth of the river with five large and eight small vessels of war; when all the male inhabitants of the village, capable of bearing arms, (being 33) turned out with the Militia of the neighboring towns, to prevent his landing, leaving only two men to take the women and children into the woods, in case he should land and send a detachment of troops, as had been threatened, to burn the bridge across the river."

Henry O'Reilly, in his "Sketches of Rochester," published at Rochester in 1838, devotes over two pages to this visit of the British squadron, and while his account contains some decided errors, it is given herewith in full:

A serious alarm, attended by some amusing consequences occurred in May, 1814, when Sir James Yeo, with a fleet of thirteen vessels of various sizes appeared off the mouth of the Genesee, threatening the destruction of the rude improvements in and around Rochester. Messengers were dispatched to arouse the people in the surrounding country for defence against the threatened attack. There were then but thirty-three people in Rochester capable of bearing arms. This little band threw up a breastwork called Fort Bender, near the Deep Hollow,

**Remains of Fort Bender - 1924**

beside the Lower Falls, and hurried down to the junction of

the Genesee and Lake Ontario, five miles north of the present city limits, where the enemy threatened to land, leaving behind them two old men, with some young lads, to remove the women and children into the woods, in case the British should attempt to land for the capture of the provisions and destruction of the bridge at Rochester, etc. Francis Brown and Elisha Ely acted as captains and Issac W. Stone as major, of the Rochester forces, which were strengthened by the additions that could be made from this thinly settled region. Though the equipments and discipline of these troops would not form a brilliant picture for a warlike eye, their very awkwardness in those points, coupled as it was with their sagacity and courage, accomplished more perhaps than could have been effected by a larger force of regular troops bedizened with the trappings of military pump. The militia thus hastily collected were marched and countermarched, disappearing in the woods at one point and suddenly emerging elsewhere so as to impress the enemy with the belief that the force collected for defence, was far greater than it actually was. (The circumstances here related are substantially as mentioned to the writer by one who was then and is now a resident of Rochester). An officer with a flag of truce was sent from the British fleet. A militia officer marched down, with ten of the most soldier-like men, to receive him on Lighthouse Point. These militiamen carried their guns as nearly upright as might be consistent with their plan of being ready for action by keeping hold of the triggers! The British officer was astonished: he looked "unutterable things." "Sir," said he, "do you receive a flag of truce under arms, with cocked triggers?" "Excuse me, excuse me, Sir: we backwoodsmen are not well versed in military tactics," replied the American officer, who promptly sought to rectify his error by ordering his men to "ground arms!" The Briton was still more astonished, and, after delivering a brief message, immediately departed for the fleet, indicating that the ignorance of tactics he has witnessed was all feigned for the occasion, so as to deceive the British commodore into a snare!

Shortly afterward, on the same day, another officer came ashore with a flag of truce for a further parley, as the British were evidently too suspicious of strategem to attempt a hostile landing if there was any possibility of compromising for the spoils. Captain Francis Brown was deputed with a guard to receive the last flag of truce. The British officer

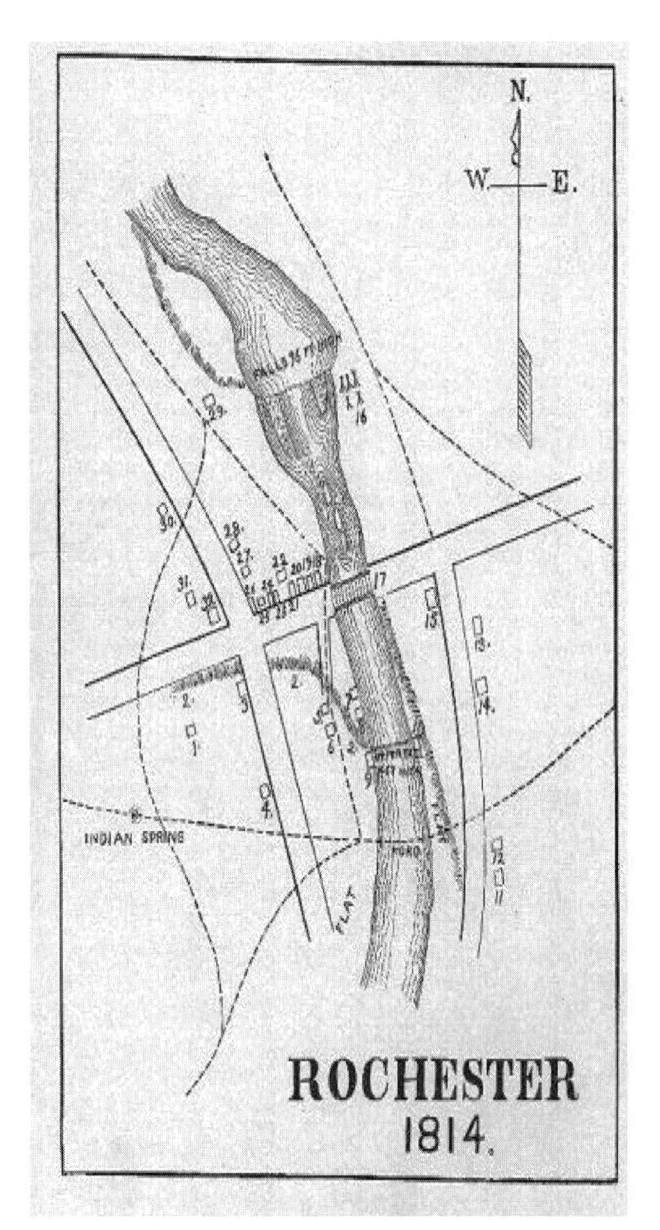

**Early Rochester map showing the bridge over the Genesee River**

looked suspiciously upon him and upon his guard; and, after some conversation, familiarly grasped the pantaloons of Captain B. about the knee, remarking, as he firmly handled it, "Your cloth is too good to be spoiled by such a bungling tailor;" alluding to the width and clumsy aspect of the garment. Brown was quick as well as resolute, and replied jocosely that" he was prevented from dressing fashionably by his haste that morning to salute such distinguished visitors!" The British obviously imagined that Brown was a regular officer of the American army, whose regimentals were masked by the clumsy overclothes. The proposition was then made, that, if the Americans would deliver up the provisions and military stores which might be in and around Rochester or Charlotte, Sir James Yeo would spare the settlements from destruction. "Will you comply with the offer?" "Blood kneedeep first!" was the emphatic reply of Francis Brown.

While this parley was in progress, an American officer, with his staff, returning from the Niagara frontier, was accidentally seen passing from one wooded point to another; and this, with other circumstances, afforded to the British "confirmation strong" that their suspicions were well founded; that there was a considerable American army collected; and that the Yankee officers shammed ignorance for the purpose of entrapping ashore the Commodore and his forces!

The return of the last flag to the fleet was followed by a vigorous attack in bombs and balls, while the compliment was spiritedly returned, not without some effect on at least one of the vessels, by a rusty old six-pounder, which had been furbished and mounted on a log for the important occasion. After a few hours spent in this unavailing manner, Admiral Yeo ran down to Pulteneyville, about twenty miles to the east of the Genesee river, where, on learning how they had been outwitted and deterred from landing by such a handful of militia, their mortification could scarcely restrain all hands from a hearty laugh at the "Yankee trick. "

O'Reilly's informant as to the events he somewhat flippantly describes could hardly have been a personal observer of them, or he would not have given the historian the "Blood knee-deep first" story, which is entirely unsubstantiated; nor would he have called the eighteen-pounder mounted near the mouth of the river, "a rusty old six-pounder."

The clearest and best account of this visit of Commodore Yeo to the Genesee is that given by Elisha Ely in the "Proceedings at the Annual Festivals of the Pioneers of Rochester" published in 1848, already referred to, and is hereby given in full, as he was an active participant in the "flag of truce" incident:

31

**Elisha Ely**

"It was soon known that the British fleet was on our own coast, and that it was at Oswego. Captain, now Colonel Stone of Porter's Volunteers, was commissioned to raise a regiment of dragoons. He had recruited about fifty men with whom he went to the mouth of the river. He directed the eighteen-pounder to be sent there and the four-pounder to Deep Hollow Bridge. On the Sabbath we threw up a breastwork on the south side of the bridge, loosened all the plank which were pinned down, and finished our work in the evening. About sundown on the 14th of May, 1814, I received a message from Colonel Stone, saying the British fleet were in sight, and requesting me to notify the inhabitants; but that we need not come until the next morning. About 11 o'clock p.m., another messenger came requesting us to come immediately. H. Ely and Co. had previously received fifty muskets and 3,000 fixed ammunition; these were distributed among the inhabitants as far as was necessary. Each man took twenty-four rounds of cartridge. At that time there were but thirty-two men in the place; one was left to cart off the women and children if necessary, and another declined to go. The cart was the only conveyance in the place. About 2 o'clock in the morning we started. It rained fast and was very dark; the roads were exceedingly muddy. We arrived at the mouth of the river soon after daylight in the midst of a fog. The lake was perfectly calm, and we could distinctly hear the British boats rowing about in various directions. An old boat was lying near which had been used as a lighter. Colonel Stone proposed to Captain Francis Brown and myself to take some men, and see if we could capture some of the British boats. Six seaman were soon found to man the oars, and twelve volunteers with muskets were stowed out of sight in the bottom of the boat. Captain Brown stood upon one thwart and myself upon another, and then with muffled oars we put to sea. At the point a sentry had been placed who hailed us. We did not answer and he fired. The ball passed between Captain Brown and myself and struck the water beyond us. We rowed on slowly and noiselessly into the lake. When we were out a mile or more, a gun was fired from shore, and soon another and another. We lay to conjecturing what it could mean. The fog was disappearing very rapidly; we soon could see Colonel Stone on his white horse, and beyond us the topmasts of the fleet which lay at anchor in a line, up and down the lake. Directly the fog had entirely disappeared, and we lay within the range of the guns of the whole fleet, seventeen sail in all. We turned and rowed slowly towards the shore. Soon a twelve-oared barge was in pursuit of us, and gained on us very rapidly. We feared they might have a swivel on board and they were so near us that we could distinctly count their oars. After a moment's consultation, we concluded to head our boat for Irondequoit. The object was to give our 18-pounder on shore an opportunity to fire upon the pursuing boat. Brown observed to me, 'Well, Ely, we shall have to go to Halifax.' I replied, 'It looks very much like it.' Jehiel Barnard, now of this place, raised his head, and with compressed lips said, 'I hope you will let us fight first.' We had not gone far towards Irondequoit before the British boat stopped. Brown observed, 'They think there is some trap.' We stopped rowing; they soon commenced again, and we too. They pulled a few strokes and then turned toward the shipping, and we to the mouth of the river. The guns from the fleet could have sunk us at any time.

"About 10 o'clock a flag of truce put off from the flagship of the enemy. Colonel Stone asked me whether I was used to receiving a flag of truce. The answer was, 'No!' Captain Brown was asked; the reply the same. Colonel Stone then told Brown and myself to do the best we could, adding, 'Don't let them come into the river—don't let them land at all—their feet shall not pollute our soil.' Up the lake, a little above the mouth of the river, a very large tree had fallen into the lake where they was sufficient water for the boat to lie alongside. We went out on the tree and tied a white handkerchief to a stick. The boat came alongside; the officer, who was in full dress and a splendid looking man, proposed going on shore. We told him our orders were positive; by this time twelve armed men made their appearance on the shore of the lake. The officer bearing the flag said, 'Is it your custom to receive a flag of truce under arms?' We told him he must excuse us, as we were not soldiers but citizens; we however requested the men to return. He then said he was commanded by his Excellency Sir James Yeo, to say that, 'if we would give up the public property, private property should be respected.' He then produced a paper signed by quite a number of citizens of Oswego, the contents of which, as near I can recollect, were that, as the government had left a large quantity of stores and munitions of war at that place, without adequate force to protect it, they would not risk their lives and property to defend it. It was arranged that Brown should stay with the flag officer and I return to our commander, Colonel Stone. I delivered the message and read the paper above alluded to, which the officer had handed me with a pledge to return it when read. Colonel Stone rose and said, 'Go back and tell them that the public property is in the hands of those who will defend it.'

"Soon after the flag had returned to the ship a gunboat was seen coming from the fleet, towed by four boats. After a short consultation Judge John Williams was requested to select twelve good riflemen and take a position under a ridge of gravel thrown up by the waves at the point on the east

**Bridge over the Genesee River**

side of the river. A small boat was sent up to the turn of the river, out of sight of the enemy, to ferry the men across. Soon we saw them crossing the marsh through the tall grass and placed in the desired position—all lying on the ground, from which they were to rise on a given signal from Colonel Stone. Brown and myself were to occupy our position in the boat. Our twelve men were again selected, with six sailors to row the boat. The object was to let the gunboat get within reach of the riflemen, and then that we should go and capture her. The lieutenant having charge of the cannon has positive orders from Colonel Stone not to fire until he was directed. By this time the gunboat was in thirty or forty rods of where we wanted her. The boats towing her opened to the right and left, and she fired a six-pound shot, which fell into the river several rods below the storehouses. The moment they fired our cannon was discharged, and with it went all our hopes. Colonel Stone was standing within ten feet of the cannon. He turned, drew his sword, and I believe would have done serious injury had not his arm been arrested. The first gun from the gunboat was evidently a trial shot. She would undoubtedly have come a little nearer the shore had we not fired, and if so we should have assuredly captured her. She was a vessel of from 90 to 100 tons, sloop rigged. I hardly know whether the incident is worth relating, but at the moment it was extremely exciting, for we considered the gunboat already our prize. She then fired fifteen or twenty sixty-eight pound shots, which did no injury except one, which struck one of the storehouses. Where they struck the ground they turned up a deep furrow, sometimes several rods in length. Some of the balls were used in this city a long time afterwards in breaking stone for buildings.

"Soon after this occurrence General Porter arrived. About 4 o'clock p.m. another flag was seen coming from the fleet. General Porter sent Major Darby Noon, his aide, to receive it. The demand then was that if the property was not surrendered he would land his army and 400 Indians and take it. General Porter answered that if he chose to send his troops and Indians ashore, we would take care of them, and that if they sent another flag he would fire upon it. General Porter appeared to be very indignant at the threat contained in the message from the enemy.

"Perhaps I ought to mention that Colonel Hopkins called out his regiment. Some companies came from the west side of the river, and many in small parties, so that the second day at night we had 600 or 800 men. There was plenty of pork, flour, and whiskey, but nothing else, and we were without utensils for cooking. I well recollect Esq. Scranton as belonging to the same mess with me. We used to mix flour and cold water in little cakes and bake them on a common shovel. We toasted our pork on sticks over a fire and drank water for coffee. The thought never occurred to any of us belonging to Rochester that we could send home and get food.

"It will be recollected that at this time the temperance reformation had not begun in Western New York. It was considered quite unhealthy to drink Genesee water without whiskey; and the salt pork without vegetables made the men exceedingly thirsty. The result may readily be conceived. I saw a captain the third morning throw aside his sword and military coat and fight with one of his own men. It was a well-contested battle. The captain at length conquered his man, which was of course his undoubted right under military discipline. The third morning the fleet hoisted sail and stood down the lake, and we went to our homes."

From the pamphlet to which we are indebted for Mr. Elisha Ely's excellent narrative quoted above, the following paragraph is taken from that part of the proceedings relative to the Festival of 1847:

"Mr. Hervey Ely, who came here in 1813, gave a full account of the attack of the British upon the American works at the mouth of the river. He was one of the party who marched to the defense of the place. As our readers are familiar with this action, we must for want of space omit the particulars. Judge Sampson called upon all who were present at that engagement to rise. Messrs. Ely, Kempshall, Scrantom, Smith, Graves, and Green rose."

In 1851, three years after the publication of the pamphlet containing Elisha Ely's account of the British "flag of truce" incident, Orsamus Turner published in Rochester his well-known "History of the Pioneer Settlement of Phelps & Gorham's Purchase." In this work he devotes over two pages to the incident under discussion, and his account is evidently based almost entirely upon Ely's narrative. The only additional information given by Turner is quoted from page 518 of his work:

In addition to the force of Captain Stone, there was stationed at Charlotte a volunteer company, under command of Captain Frederick Rowe; the men principally citizens of what are now the towns of Gates and Greece; and Colonel

Atkinson's regiment, from what are now the northwestern towns of Monroe county, were either there previously or as soon as the exigency required. The only fortification at Charlotte was a breastwork upon the bluff, near the old hotel, so located as to command the road leading up the bank to the wharf. It was composed of two tiers of ship timber with a space between the tiers filled in with barn manure.

Neither William F. Peck in his "Semi-Centennial History of the City of Rochester" (Syracuse, 1884), or in his contribution to the "Landmarks of Monroe County" (Boston, 1895), nor Jenny Marsh Parker in her "Rochester: A Story Historical" (Rochester, 1884), adds anything authentic to Ely's or Turner's narrative. But the latter writers base their accounts either directly or indirectly, it would appear, upon O'Reilly and Turner, quoting from both.

An article in the Rochester "Post Express" of December 18, 1897, signed W.H.S. and dealing with the various appearances of Commodore Yeo off the Genesee, gives an interesting and pertinent letter from Brigadier-General Porter to Governor Tompkins, concerning the last appearance of the British fleet. Porter's letter is as follows:

Canandaigua, May 17, 1814.

Sir: I returned yesterday with Major Noon from the mouth of the Genesee river, where we were called on Friday last by information of the approach of the British fleet.

We saved the town and our credit by fairly outbullying John Bull. The discovery that we had troops, without knowing their number, concealed in a ravine near the mouth of the river to cut off their retreat in case they entered it, together with the tone of the defiance with which we answered their demands (the last answered having been conveyed by our friend Major Noon), made them think it prudent to be off. We had, however, some excellent officers and good men well prepared, and in case the enemy had landed I had no doubt of a result creditable to the state.

When the enemy left Genesee they stood to the eastward, and a cannonading has been heard in the direction of Pultneyville, whither I believe General Swift has proceeded with some volunteers and militia.

P.B. Porter, Brig-Gen.

General Porter's letter and Mr. Ely's reminiscences appear to be the only first-hand reports by eye-witnesses of the locally famous events of May 14-16, 1814.

There has been much discussion as to why Sir James Yeo did not land a force and take such supplies as he wanted from those on hand at the mouth of the river. The probabilities are that he did not consider the "game worth the candle," as he had much more important work to do, either in blockading Commodore Chauncey's squadron at Sacketts Harbor, or preparing to meet him on the lake. At all events there is no further record of Yeo's appearance off the Genesee.

**Peter B. Porter**

A large portion of the American fleet, however, did appear there once more, when on September 22, 1814, it arrived with 3,000 men under Major-General Izard. This force left Sacketts Harbor on the 21st, and after being taken to the Genesee Rriver by Chauncey's squadron, proceeded to Batavia. The incident is reported to the secretary of war by General Izard in a letter dated "Northern Army Headquarters, Batavia, September 28, 1814." It is taken from an article in the Rochester "post Express" of December 18, 1897, and signed W.H.S. and is as follows:

> On the 21st instant the fleet under Commodore Chauncey sailed the forenoon from Sacketts Harbor, and the wind favoring us, we were off the mouth of the Genesee river the next morning early. The troops were all disembarked before night and encamped near the lake. Every exertion was used to collect a sufficient number of wagons and horses for the transportation of our camp equipage and provisions, but our appearance being unexpected, and that part of the country thinly peopled, it was not until the 24th that we could resume our march. Part of the tents and stores were unavoidably left, to follow as fast as means could be procured for that purpose.

Through excessively bad roads and amidst continual and heavy rains we proceeded, the officers of every grade, with very few exceptions, being dismounted. On the 26th, some hours before night, the whole of our corps arrived in good spirits at this village, and with a less proportion of men disabled for immediate duty than could under such circumstances have been expected.

**General Izard**

General Izard's force marched up the west side of the river as far as the Ridge road, and then went along that road until it struck off to the left for Batavia. Meanwhile the American fleet returned down the lake to Sackett's Harbor or to blockade the British fleet in Kingston.

So far as available sources of information show this was the last appearance of a naval force at the mouth of the Genesee River during the War of 1812.

# The War of 1812 on the Genesee River: A Documentary Journey

In 1788, Oliver Phelps obtained the rights to the land along the Genesee River. Phelps negotiated with the Iroquois to let him build a mill there where the Indians could bring their grain to grind. This swath of land on both sides of the river became an important trading area with trans-shipment points being established at the upper falls and at the junction of the river with Lake Ontario.[4] From there goods were sent in ships or barges to Canada. In 1802, Genesee County was formed from part of Ontario County, using the Genesee River as the boundary line. Monroe County was later formed from portions of both counties, straddling the Genesee River. When war against the British was declared on June 28, 1812, the city of Rochester did not exist and the area that was to become Rochester had a population of only 15.

The village of Charlotte, at the junction of the Genesee River and Lake Ontario, was an important trading post along the lake and gained its own customs agent in 1805. Some shipbuilding was conducted along the river where the deeper waters of the river made it a more suitable location for such an endeavor than Irondequoit Bay, just east of the river. The maritime activities at Charlotte made it a strategic location during the war.

When war was declared, the brig *Oneida* was the only U.S. Navy vessel on Lake Ontario. The British squadron consisted of three ships. In order to close this gap and attempt to gain maritime superiority on the lake, the Americans commenced the purchase of merchant vessels on the lake for conversion to warships. This was a temporary measure until new vessels could be built at Sackett's Harbor.

The action at the Genesee began even before war was declared. The *Oneida*, under the command of Lieutenant Melancthon T.

---

[4] O. Turner, History of the Pioneer Settlement of Phelp's and Gorham's Purchase and Morris' Reserve, Rochester: William Alling, 1851, p. 139.

Woolsey, conducted frequent patrols of the southern shore of the lake in an effort to ensure the safety of the region and to continue to enforce customs requirements. On one such occasion, Woolsey hit the jackpot. His report to Secretary of the Navy Paul Hamilton summarizes it best:

> I have the honor to inform you that I sailed on the 3rd Instant on a Cruise to the Westward-On the 4th (off Pultney Ville) discovered three sail to windward apparently standing in for Genesee River – gave chase to them, but night coming on and the weather being too hazy to run in the mouth of the river hawld off shore for the night under short sail- At day light on the 5th discovered two schooners (supposed to be two of the three we chased the day before) standing in for the land – At 7P.M. we brought to one of the Schooners which proved to be the *Lord Nelson* from Prescot (a port

**USS *Scourge* – former *Lord Nelson***

> opposite Ogdensburgh on the St Lawrence) said to be bound to Newark in Canada, she had no papers on board other than a loose Journal and a bill of lading of a part of her Cargo, but no Register, licence or clearance., Wether it was intended to smuggle her cargo on our shores, or wether she was hovering along our shore to take on board property for the Canada market in violation of the Embargo law I was not able to determine- But appearances were such as to warrant a suspicion of an intention to smuggle both ways- I accordingly took her Crew out and sent her with my gunner on board as Prize Master to this port. After dispatching her I stood off shore in chase of the other Schooner which the

Master of the *Lord Nelson* informed me was the *Mary Hatt*, also a British schooner, but finding that she had crossed the Line- I hove up for this port in order to lay up the Prize and make my report to the Department. All the proofs which I can collect respecting her voyage I will transmit without delay to the District Attorney.[5]

*Lord Nelson* was purchased in Prize Court and added to the American fleet as the *Scourge*.

While Woolsey tried to maintain security on the lake, the militia made attempts to improve security along the shores. In a report to Governor Thompkins, New York Militia Major General Amos Hall reported: "We are very much engaged at present in making necessary arrangements for general defense...I have ordered a company to be stationed at Sodus and Pulteneyville and one company at the mouth of the Genesee River."[6] Despite these attempts, defenses remained largely non-existent at many of the vulnerable points along the shore. Militia General Peter B. Porter bluntly reported to Thompkins:

> We have been daily amused for two months with news of the approach of heavy ordnance, of flying artillery, of regular troops, &c., &c., to this frontier, but none have arrived. They come to Utica and then disappear. They timidly dance backward and forward in the interior of the country, without knowing what to do or being of service anywhere. The Genesee River, Sodus, Oswego, and the brig at Sackett's Harbor, are all alternately to be defended, as a British ship appears to pass from one end of the lake to the other. This miserable and timid system of defense must be abandoned, or the nation is ruined and disgraced. Make a bold push at any one point and you will find your enemy, give them as much business as they can attend to at Niagara and at Ogdensburg, and you will not see them groping among the marshes of Sodus to pillage the miserable huts of the poor

---

[5] Woolsey to Hamilton, June 9, 1812, in William S. Dudley and Michael J. Crawford, eds., Naval War of 1812, A Documentary History, 3 vols., Washington, DC: Naval Historical Center, 1985, 1992, 2002; vol 1, p. 274. Hereafter Naval War and volume.

[6] Major General Amos Hall to Governor Thompkins, June 29, 1812, in Ernest Cruikshank, ed., The Documentary History of the Campaign upon the Niagara Frontier, Reprint, Arno Press Inc., 1971; 1812: 1, p. 80. Hereafter Documents.

inhabitants. But it is needless for me to say more; my views have been long known.[7]

Efforts at protecting the frontier continued over the next several months with varied success. Forces, both regular army and militia, were needed to effect the invasion of Canada along the Niagara Frontier and could not be spared elsewhere. The British, however, did not make a bold move on the southern shore of Lake Ontario until September. This move was more accidental, rather than intentional. As Major General Van Rensselear reported to Major General Dearborn,

> The day after the termination of the armistice the *Royal George* and another vessel chased some vessels returning from Niagara to Oswego into the Genesee River and fired a few shot. This has excited an alarm among the inhabitants, and, according to the custom prevailing on the whole frontier, they have sent a deputation to me praying protection. I have ordered them some ammunition; I can do no more.[8]

Van Rensselear's focus was on preventing a British invasion along the Niagara Frontier and kept the troops occupied to the west. Although he was primarily in charge of the land forces, Van Rensselear did little to provide any support to the naval effort on the lakes. Lt. Jesse D. Elliott at Buffalo was more aware of the need to get more vessels on the lakes armed. He looked at the ships in the Genesee River as the next additions to the Lake Ontario fleet. He ordered the carpenters destined for Black Rock to Genesee Falls where he would "get on altering the Vessels until I have your further Commands. Should arming these Vessels meet your approbation, the ordnance had better immediately come on to that place together with the officers and men."[9] The conversion of merchant vessels did little to instill confidence for those ashore. Van Rensselear later reported that:

> The alarm which lately took place in the County of Ontario by the enemy's ships chasing some vessels into the mouth of the Genesee River, has induced Judge Atwater to make a communication to me of a very unpleasant nature. After stating the great zeal with which the militia turned out, he says, "but sir, I lament when I tell you that neither arms nor ammunition are provided for these brave men; no, not

---

[7] Porter to Thompkins, August 30, 1812, <u>Documents</u>, 1812:1, p. 224.

[8] Van Rensselear to Dearborn, September 12, 1812, <u>Documents</u>, 1812:1, p. 252.

[9] Elliott to Chauncey, September 14, 1812, <u>Naval War</u>, 1: 313.

one musket to six men that would cheerfully risk their lives in defence of their country." He says, "they are destitute of arms and ammunition; they are neither of them to be purchased in the county."[10]

Meanwhile, the conversion of the ships at Genesee never materialized. As Van Rensselear reported to Governor Thompkins:

> I ordered Lieut. Elliott of the navy, with the men engaged for the service under his command, to the mouth of the Genesee River to arm and equip such vessels lately blockaded these, as he might think proper for the public service. He has undoubtedly advised Captain Chauncey of the arrangement. But, since the departure of Lieut. Elliott, I have been informed that those vessels have escaped from Genesee River and gone to Oswego.[11]

As Van Rensselear speculated, Elliott did indeed inform Chauncey of his intent to convert the vessels at the Genesee. An abstract from the Journal of Commodore Isaac Chauncey details the following:

> Received by Express a letter from lieut Elliott and sent a copy of it to the Honorable The Secretary.
>
> In answer same day directed him by Express, to proceed in altering the Vessels in Genessee he mentioned as fit for our purposes.
>
> In consequence of the information communicated by lieut Elliott directed The Storekeeper to change the destination of 2-24 pdrs-10-6 pdres-10-4 pdrs with everything necessary for them, with musket, pistols &c for 100 men, from Buffaloe to Genessee River.
>
> Directed Capt [Richard] Smith commanding the detachment of Marines to proceed, and keep them together until his arrival at Rome, there to divide them, placing one half under command of lieut [Charles] Hanna with orders to proceed to Genessee River: with orders to proceed himself to Sacketts' Harbor.

---

[10] Van Rensselear to Thompkins, September 15, 1812, Documents, 1812:1, p. 266.

[11] Van Rennselear to Thompkins, September 22, 1812, Documents, 1812:1, p. 286-287.

> Sept 24 Ordd lieut [John] Pettigrew of the John Adams to proceed with the detachment under his command to Genessee River
>
> [Sept] 26th  Set off Sacketts' Harbor leaving orders for capt Ludlow to forward the Sails, rigging, blocks, anchors, cables &c &c to be prepared and fitted, to Sacketts' Harbor, for a Brig and 3 gun boats: also sails, rigging, blocks, &c for 3 gun boats to be sent to Genessee River.[12]

It wouldn't be long before the British returned to the Genesee. On October 2, 1812, a raiding party from the *Royal George* landed at the mouth of the Genesee. Their objective was clear—the marine stores located in a warehouse near the river. Local citizens reported:

> We are informed that a British armed vessel entered the mouth of the Genesee River on the 2nd inst. And cut out a sloop, (the *Lady Murray*) and the United States revenue cutter: that they landed about 80 men and demanded the warehouse to be opened to take out her sails and rigging, of which she was dismantled, as we suppose, by the collector of the port having been seized last fall for smuggling and afterwards bonded.
>
> They destroyed no property and took none, but what was of use to them for marine purposes.
>
> They appear to be determined to command the lakes. It is conjectured by some that Captain Wm. McKinstry of Penfield, the owner, was privy to it because the vessel was seized from him and was likely to be condemned, and because he was ordered out to Niagara when he hesitated to go, wishing to have a force posted at the river.
>
> There were three or four vessels taken four miles up the river to the upper landing a week or two before and dismantled, which the British did not offer to take. It is said the inhabitants had not a charge of powder to defend themselves.[13]

A letter to the editor of the New York Gazette from an officer of the 13th Regiment corroborated the story. He identified the British vessel as

---

[12] Journal of Commodore Isaac Chauncey. Naval War, 1: 317.

[13] Oliver L. Phelps, Freeman Atwater, and J. Howley to Governor Thompkins, October 4, 1812, Documents, 1812:2, p. 32-33.

the *Royal George* which "landed about fifty men, under the pretence of searching for deserters. They plundered the inhabitants of every valuable article they could find and departed before the people could collect to resist them, taking with them two American vessels."[14] An article in the New York Evening Post presents another view of this incident:

> On Thursday night last a boat with forty men and a barge with thirty men, from the British brig *Royal George,* which lay off, came into the mouth of the Genesee River and cut away the fastenings of two vessels and towed them out without any opposition. One of them was a schooner, the *Lady Murray,* owned by Captain Wm. McKinstry of Penfield in this county, the other a small vessel used as a United States revenue cutter. The next evening the British boat returned to the store house of Mr. Spalding and required the sails and rigging belonging to the schooner, which had been dismantled. Finding they were in the store house they entered and took them. They were also about taking a barrel of whiskey, but on Mr. Spalding telling them it was private property and that he would give them two gallons to drink, they departed declaring that they wished to take nothing but vessels or such other property as would lessen our means of operating against them.

**Royal George** pursued by the **American fleet**

According to the information given by a man who deserted from the British boat on Thursday night, the *Royal George* left Newark four days previous with a view of taking out the above vessels, well knowing, it would seem, that we had no force there to prevent it.

On the preceding evening the *Royal George,* had sent her boats into Irondequoit Bay, mistaking it for the river, and

---

[14] Letter to the editor of the New York Gazette from an officer of the 13th Regiment, October 4, 1812, Documents, 1812:2, p. 33.

discovering some men fishing, hailed them. The fishermen, understanding they were British and in want of a pilot, extinguished their lights and made for the shore, whereupon the British fired on them and wounded one man in the arm. They pursued the fishermen a short distance in the woods and one of their sailors, finding himself on *terra firma,* deserted from them. He states that the captain of the *Royal George* intended to make another visit and endeavor to cut out some boats laying higher up the river. Some apprehensions are entertained for the boats lately sent from Oswego with arms and ammunition for our troops at Niagara.[15]

It is interesting to see the disparity in the number of troops that came ashore from account to account. Although the suspected involvement of McKinstry in informing the British about the location of the supplies has never been firmly established, the British apparently were somehow aware of the presence of the vessels in the river and the state of defenses in the area. Hanford does not make any reference to this incident. This was the last visit by the British to the Genesee River in 1812.

The few residents of the area were naturally anxious about the war. Edwin Scrantom, one of the first residents along the Genesee River, commented, "The year 1813 came in laden with tales of war and bloodshed, and gradually the subject of war became the all-absorbing one, and the question in Western New York was ... how shall we keep the little beginnings from destruction, and our familieies together during the war..."[16] The first visit of 1813 came in June at it too, was a raiding expedition. Such actions were either designed to weaken the American forces by capturing all their provisions and stores, or were a sign of inadequate supplies in Canada forcing the British to seek alternate sources. It was likely both. An article appearing in Rochester History in the Fall of 1991 titled "Genesee River During the War of 1812" by Lillian Roemer provides ample documentation to support the lack of supplies in Canada. Poulson's American Daily Advertiser of Philadelphia was the first to cover the incident:

> The enemy visited the mouth of the Genesee River yesterday morning and took about 500 barrels of provisions

---

[15] New York Evening Post, October 14, 1812, Documents, 1812:2, p. 35.

[16] Harriett Julia Naylor, ed., "And This War Rochester! Excerpts from the Old Citizen No. 1, p. 7-8.Letters of Edwin Scrantom," Rochester History, Vol IV (January 1942), No. 1, p. 7-8.

and 1700 bushels of corn, as is said by a person who is from there this day. Apprehensions are entertained of a similar visit at Sodus and Oswego, and Colonel Swift's volunteer regiment has marched to the former place to-day. On their passage from the Head of the Lake several boats have been taken. Five laden with provisions are named among the number taken on Sunday.[17]

Poulson's later gave a more detailed account of the activity in the region:

> The naval force of the enemy on Lake Ontario are cruising from Niagara down the American side of that lake for the purpose, it would seem, of sweeping the coast, in which they were but too successful. On Saturday, the 12th inst., near the Eighteen Mile Creek, they captured two schooners and several boats, with valuable cargoes, bound from Oswego to Niagara. On Tuesday, the 15th inst., at 4 p.m., the force appeared off the mouth of the Genesee River, to which place they sent several boats, with about 300 men, 150 of whom landed, went into the village of Charlotte, placed sentries around the place to prevent the inhabitants from going out to give the alarm, and proceeded to execute their object. They entered the storehouse and took off between 400 and 500 barrels of flour, pork, etc., together with a large boat laden with 1200 bushels of corn, destined for our troops at Niagara. About 80 of the militia of Penfield turned out, but did not arrive in season for service. The enemy went off about 4 next morning, having met with no opposition except from the owners of the boat, Messrs. Spalding and Hildreth.
>
> From this they proceeded to Sodus, before which they appeared on Saturday last, about 5 p. m., and sent a demand for the property there to be delivered up, accompanied with a threat to burn the place if refused. The property had been removed to a safe distance, and the enemy, being disappointed, executed their threat on Sunday by setting fire to several buildings. We have heard of but one man killed, Ab. Warren.
>
> On the first alarm, Colonel Swift's regiment of militia was ordered out, but reaching the point of attack before the enemy appeared were dismissed. They have, however, been

---

[17] Poulson's American Daily Advertiser, June 20, 1813, Documents, 1813:2, p. 93.

called out again, and we understand the artillery under Captain Rees and infantry of Captain A. Dox of Geneva have turned out with alacrity highly commendable.

P. S.—We have just heard that the enemy evacuated Sodus on Sunday afternoon, having burnt several valuable buildings belonging to Messrs. Merril, Wycan and others, and destroyed or carried about 800 barrels of flour, &c.[18]

Lt Woolsey reported to Commodore Chauncey that "The fleet consists of the *Wolfe*, *Royal George*, *Earl Moria*, *Prince Regent*, *Simcoe*, one gunboat, and a prize schooner lately taken by them at Genesee River with Mr. Hooker's goods onboard. I have no doubt but that these boats which have just joined the fleet have been to the Ducks to land a part of the boats, with which their ships were deeply laden before they left Genesee River."[19]

The Genesee River was not the only target of raids. Just about any location on the southern shore of Lake Ontario was vulnerable to attack. The next victim was the village of Sodus. Commodore Yeo relayed this summary of his raids to the Admiralty:

...on the 13th. We captured two Schooners, and some Boats, going to the Enemy with Supplies, by them I received information, that there was a Depot of Provisions, at Genesee River, I accordingly proceeded off that River, landed some Seaman, and Marines of the Squadron, and brought off all the Provisions found in the Government Stores, as also a sloop laden with Grain, for the Army, on the 19th. I anchored off the great Sodus, landed a party of the 1st. Regiment of Royal Scotts, and took off six hundred Barrels of Flour, and Pork, which had arrived there for their Army.[20]

Poulson's provided this report of the raid on Sodus from Montreal:

We understand by a report from the Upper Province that Sir James Yeo when he was last out landed a small part of his force at Sodus, a village belonging to the enemy, where with trifling loss he captured about 300 barrels of pork and a considerable quantity of clothing. The provisions he sent

---

[18] Poulson's American Daily Advertiser, June 30, 1813, Documents, 1813:2, p. 93-94.

[19] Woolsey to Chauncey, June 19, 1813, Documents, 1813:3, p. 269.

[20] Yeo to First Secretary of the Admiralty John W. Croker, June 29, 1813, Naval War, 2: 498.

> immediately to General Vincent, who with his gallant little army has entirely prevented the further advance of the American army into the Province.
>
> In addition to the number of boats with provisions and stores taken and destroyed by the squadron and advance of Brigadier-General Vincent's army on the 6th and 10th inst., we have much pleasure in stating that by letters from Kingston of the 16th inst., received in town on Saturday evening, Sir James Yeo had returned to that place after having completely scoured the lake, and entering all the creeks and bays on the enemy's side, and capturing four American schooners having on board 400 barrels of pork and a quantity of merchandise intended for the enemy's army at Fort George. Four companies of the Royals were embarked on board of the fleet to serve as marines, and were to sail from Kingston on Thursday last. The enemy's fleet was then still in Sackett's Harbor.[21]

Captain Woolsey, writing to Commodore Chauncey, highlighted the preparations the local populous took to defend themselves from future raids. Unfortunately, the militia generally only responded when there was a viable threat nearby, and generally left once the threat had abated. No permanent defenses existed to counter the British threat.

> The British Squadron landed yesterday morning a body of men at Great Sodus and burned it. I think this savage warfare calls for revenge. A Dr. Baldwin and a Captain Tappen have just got in here from Sodus, which place they left about 11 o'clock this morning. At that time the fleet appeared to be about Pultneyville. Mr. Vaughan informs me that 3 more guns are on the way; how far back he does not know. I am busily employed building a battery to mount 7 guns. This place is in a wretched state of defense. The militia are all returning home, and between 2 and 300 regulars are by no means competent to defend it.[22]

New York Militia Brigadier-General William Bennett reported on the response of the militia to Governor Tompkins and detailed the defenses in the region:

---

[21] Poulson's American Daily Advertiser, July 22, 1813, Documents, 1813:2, p. 94-95.

[22] Woolsey to Chauncey, June 21, 1813, Documents, 1813:3, p. 271. Also found in Naval War, 2: 497.

On the evening of the 15th inst. I received information by express that the enemy had landed at the Genesee River and committed some depredations and were steering for Sodus Bay, where considerable public property was stored. I ordered out Lieut.-Colonel Swift's regiment and part of Major Granger's rifle battalion, who marched on Wednesday. Captain Dorsey's company of exempts marched at the same time and under my direction removed the public property to the safest place which time and the country afforded, and dismissed the troops on Saturday morning. On the evening of Sunday an express arrived that the enemy's fleet had anchored off Sodus and were preparing to land. I immediately ordered those who had not proceeded with me to return and despatched an officer for the remainder. But the enemy had effected a landing before more than 40 or 50 men arrived, who, though provided only with a few cartridges, engaged with them, but owing to the darkness of the night and the superior force of the enemy were obliged to fall back to the place where the stores were secreted. We had four men wounded, one since dead. The enemy, as I am informed by the officer of the flag, on the next day had 7 men killed. In the meantime I had ordered out Lieut.-Colonel Howell's regiment, Major Rogers' battalion and Captain Rea's company of artillery, who arrived on the two following days. A number of volunteers arrived at the same time, part from Colonel Dobbin's regiment, Seneca county. On Sunday morning they set fire to and destroyed six buildings and soon after embarked and left the shore, taking with them, as I am informed by Mr. Merril, about 230 barrels of flour, a few barrels of whiskey and pork, principally private property, and then demanded the surrender of the public property and a deserter, whom they would exchange for one they had taken along shore, which was immediately refused. I ordered Lieut.-Colonel Howell's regiment and Major Rogers' battalion to Pultneyville, whither the enemy steered their course, and had previously ordered part of Lieut.-Colonel Colt's to Sodus and dismissed Colonel Swift's, they having been on duty for some time. The property saved to the public consists of about 800 barrels of flour and pork and is now sufficiently secured from the enemy, having ordered a guard to remain and protect it. The returns of the number of men have not yet been made, but will be immediately attended to and sent to Your Excellency.

The season of the year now is so important to farmers, who compose the greater part of our country, has proved to be such a loss to those ordered out by leaving their business, that some provision in this case will be necessary to be made, and for the teams that removed the public property. The alacrity with which the *citizen soldiers* obeyed the call of their country in its defence cannot be too highly commended. The enemy, too well aware of the patriotism of our citizens, left their situation without effecting their greatest purpose, the taking or destruction of our stores, before 150 men had arrived.[23]

An interesting account of the raid comes from a Master James Richardson, a member of the Provincial Marine and Royal Navy. Richardson was part of the raiding party at Sodus and described the event in a memoir:

Our Commodore, in the absence of something to fight, proceeded to inspect the enemies' coasts and harbors in search of provisions, and being informed that the United States had a large stock of flour, deposited in the village of Big Sodus about 30 miles west of Oswego, he brought his squadron to anchor, and toward evening sent in the boats with a few sailors and detachment of about 60 of the Royals. It became dark before we made the landing, and an advance party of fifteen, of which I was one, commanded by Captain Mulcaster, proceeded at once to the village, under guidance of one acquainted with the place.

We found the houses deserted, and not a person to be seen, but one in a tavern so drunk that we could get no information from him. After seeking in vain for the inhabitants, during which strict orders were given not to molest any furniture or private property, and while our Captain was consulting as to future proceedings, it being very dark, someone hailed us from some bushes close by. Captain Mulcaster answered "Friend", but before the word was fully out, they fired a volley, which felled five of our fifteen. They then took themselves off. The detachment of the Royals coming up in our rear, having heard the firing,

---

[23] William Bennett to Governor Thompkins, June 26, 1813, <u>Documents</u>, 1813:2 p. 154-55.

took us for the enemy, and also discharged a few shots at us before the mistake was discovered.

Captain Wilson of the Royals who was among the fifteen in advance, wore a peculiarly-shaped cocked hat, which a flash of lightning, happily for our party, revealed and showed whom we were.

The enemy was mo more seen during the night, but towards morning some stragglers came within the line of our sentry and were arrested. Being questioned as to the firing, as also, where the inhabitants of the village were, they said that the inhabitants themselves fired; that on approach of the ships in the evening, a consultation was held in the village and while some would have remained quietly at home, under the conviction that they would not be molested, the majority decided to arm themselves and fire on us, some of them remarking that they would have the satisfaction of killing some British anyway.

This word having come to the Commodore he ordered the place to be burnt, as a warning to all others along the coast.

The prisoners being liberated, were instructed to say that wherever we came, if the inhabitants remained quiet, private property and rights would be respected, but, in all cases, where the people made armed resistance and wantonly fired on us, they might expect to be punished in like manner.

All we got in return for our visit was about 500 barrels of flour, found in a storehouse.

I have since conversed with an American gentleman, who was at this place at the time, who said that about 8,000 barrels of flour belonging to the United States were concealed in the woods, which were not discovered because of the blackness of the night.[24]

Bennett wasn't the only one concerned with the ill defenses and the potential for future raids. Caleb Hopkins of Canandaigua reported:

There is about $30,000 worth of public property lying at the upper landing on the Genesee river, (4 miles from its

---

[24] Robert Malcomson, ed., <u>Sailors of 1812: Memoirs and letters of Naval Officers on Lake Ontario</u>, Youngstown, NY: Old Fort Niagara Association, 1997, p. 34-37.

mouth,) consisting of pork, flour, corn, hay, &c., also a large quantity lying at Gerundgut (Irondequoit) landing, also, I am informed, there is some lying at Pulteneyville, and there was some at Sodus but it was lately destroyed.

All this property is exposed to destruction by British naval enterprise from Lake Ontario.

They have visited the mouth of Genesee river already, but were repulsed by a few militia and from their fears of there being more of them. We were then informed by a deserter from them that it was their intention to have proceeded up the river at daylight next morning and burn the stores at the upper landing.

I am now informed that on their way to the river they took a sailor on the lake by the name of William Howell, (who formerly sailed under Captain Eddes of Oswego,) and they now use him as a pilot for their excursions around the south shore of the lake; that the British Commodore keeps him on board his ship, who threatens to make another visit to the port of Genesee for the purpose of destroying the property there and also of destroying the new bridge about 7 miles from the mouth of the river, having been informed that our principal baggage waggons cross it and take the Ridge Road to Niagara.

I have been induced from my own suggestions and the advice of friends to communicate the circumstances to you, with a suggestion for you to give orders for posting a competent guard along the shore of the lake at the principal places of deposit until Commodore Chauncey shall settle the question with the British squadron respecting the superiority of the lake. Of this we have confident hopes it will be decided in a month.

Under the present circumstances no militia officer feels himself disposed to assume the responsibility without higher orders. Indeed there is a great want of ammunition and arms, and when an express is sent for them to Canandaigua under an alarm the keeper of the arsenal cannot deliver them out until a tour of 12 miles is made to obtain General Hall's order for them.

> I should state the number of 300 men to be necessary to be stationed at Genesee river in order to insure its safety and the proportional number at Gerundgut, &c.[25]

The British, naturally, were all agog over the raids, particularly the ease in which they were facilitated. Sir George Prevost made this report to Earl Bathurst:

> After the squadron under Commodore Sir James Yeo had shewn itself off the Forty Mile Creek, which principally determined the enemy to retreat from that position, it was very successfully employed in interrupting and cutting off their supplies going from the Genesee river and their other settlements upon the southern shore of the lake. Five small vessels with provisions, clothing and other articles were taken and several loaded boats were destroyed.[26]

The United States Gazette of Philadelphia, even gave the superiority of Lake Ontario to the British:

> The British fleet is now out and has command of Lake Ontario. It consists of two ships, a brig and two schooners, all of which were cruising off here on the 13th and 14th instant. It has committed many depredations on our side of the lake, particularly in the Genesee river, where a great quantity of public stores were taken. Our fleet is expected here about the first of July and is now only waiting for a large new ship, which will be ready for sea by that time in Sackett's Harbor.[27]

Despite the apparent British superiority, the United States continued its shipbuilding efforts in order to even the playing field. On September 11, 1813, the two fleets met off the Genesee River.

> I have no doubt but a decisive battle has been fought this day on the lake between Chauncey and Yeo. I heard the firing for several hours in the direction of Sodus or Genesee

---

[25] Caleb Hopkins to Governor Tompkins, July 1, 1813, Documents, 1813:2, p. 169-170.

[26] Sir George Pevost to Earl Bathurst. July 3, 1813, Documents, 1813:2, p. 176.

[27] United States Gazette, July 8, 1813, Documents, 1813:2, p. 51.

River. I believe the facts stated in the enclosed hand-bill may be relied on.[28]

**Painting of the Battle on Lake Ontario**

Captain Arthur Sinclair of the General Pike offers a first hand account of the action:

> On the 10th we pushed him so hard that he made down the Lake. We overtook him off Genesee River by his getting becalmed and our bringing the breeze up to him. He had every sail out, and was towing and sweeping to get off. This Ship lead the van and was the only one which got in good striking distance. We had warm work of it for between five and six hours and had our Schooners done their duty we must have had him. The time was calm and smooth and just suited for them; but they are commanded by a set of boys without the least experience or judgement. The Ship Madison and Brig Oneida having carronades were of no service. My ship was much cut in sails and rigging and six or seven shot in the hull – only one many slightly wounded – and we were the only one touched. He was very much cut as we could then see and have since learned.[29]

---

[28] General George McClure to Governor Thompkins, September 10, 1813, Documents, 1813:3, p. 113.

[29] Arthur Sinclair to Jack Sinclair, October 10, 1813, in Malcomson, Sailors of 1812, p. 59.

That engagement proved indecisive. Although the balance of sea power was beginning to settle out between the two adversaries, the United States recognized the value of the Lake Ontario Squadron in rapidly moving troops across the theater. When the need to move the army from Sackett's Harbor to Niagara arose, the Navy responded.

> The Honourable the Secretary at War having requested that I would afford transport to that part of the army now under the command of Colonel Scott and believed to be at or near the mouth of the Genesee River, I shall therefore proceed immediately with the squadron under my command for Genesee River, take on board Colonel Scott and his men and join you at Grenadier Island as soon as possible.[30]

That need never materialized and Commodore Chauncey continued to patrol the lake in search of an engagement with the British.

> Since I wrote you this morning, I have received a letter from the Hon. The Secretary at War, which, in consequence of the information received from you, makes it unnecessary for the fleet to proceed to the mouth of the Genesee River for Colonel Scott. I shall therefore cruise in this vicinity and in the Kingston channel until the army is ready to move for its ulterior object. I beg to repeat to you, sir, that I am now, as I always have been, ready to co-operate with the army, with the force under my command to the full extent of its power in any enterprise against the enemy.[31]

Chauncey later reported:

> After the squadron was under way yesterday for the purpose of proceeding to Genesee River to take on board Colonel Scott and the men under his command, I received a note from General Armstrong (a copy of which is enclosed) saying it would be unnecessary for me to proceed to the Genesee River at this time, but requests that I would afford the necessary protection to the army in its passage to Grenadier Island. I accordingly took my station about these islands [Ducks], which will enable me to observe any movement of the enemy at Kingston, and completely covering the movement of our army in its passage to

---

[30] Commodore Chauncey to General Wilkinson, October 16, 1813, Documents, 1813:4, p. 69-70.

[31] Commodore Chauncey to General Wilkinson, October 16, 1813, Documents, 1813:4, p. 72.

Grenadier Island, which I hope will not occupy more that two days.[32]

As the 1813 sailing season came to a close, the British and Americans both turned to shipbuilding in order to tip the balance and obtain the command of the lake. Although both fleets were wintered in their respective harbors, it did not prevent the alarm of the frenzied citizens along the river.

I have been driven home by an alarm that the British had arrived at Genesee River and were approaching this place. A levy en masse of the militia is ordered as far east as Cayuga, and our court martial, then in session at Auburn was broke up.

P.S. There are neither arms nor ammunition here. The mail has not arrived, but accounts received since I wrote the above go to confirm the general opinion that the fort is taken. At all events something must be done immediately. The militia called out have returned home because the enemy were not at Genesee River. The draft of 1000 men goes on very slowly; 600 men will not be mustered. So we go.[33]

As the war continued into 1814, a deserter from the United States by the name of Constant Bacon provided the British with the following account of the locations of stores along the southern coast of Lake Ontario:

.... The nearest depot of provisions to those already mentioned is at the mouth of the Genesee River and at the upper landing, exactly four miles, up to which place large schooners can sail. There are there large quantities of beef, pork, salt, and whiskey, and no batteaux, guns, or troops for their protection. The next, consisting of flour, pork, and whiskey, is at Irondiquet, a few miles further to the eastward. It is exactly four miles from the falls of the Genesee to the Irondiquet storehouse, and three miles from the upper landing to the falls. The country here is not well settled. The next depot is at Putney, which is between the Genesee River

---

[32] Chauncey to William Jones, October 17, 1813, Documents, 1813:4, p. 75.

[33] John C. Spencer to Governor Thompkins, Dec 26, 1813, Documents, 1813:5, p. 52-54.

and Big Sodus—this depot is on the lake shore. It consists, as before, of a large quantity of provisions and salt, and there are no men stationed here, unless they have come very lately. There is also a large depot at Sodus. There is also a large depot at Oswego, but there is a strong force stationed there. A schooner of 40 or 45 tons is building at Irondiquet.[34]

New York Militia General Peter Porter recognized the importance, and vulnerability of these supplies and made several calls for additional troops to protect them, the first coming on April 8:

> Several British vessels have already been seen on Lake Ontario. The deposits of public property at Genesee River and Sodus would in my opinion render it prudent to guard each of them at present by a small force. A company of volunteers will be raised near each of these and will serve as a guard so long as they remain there. But permit me again to recommend the expediency of authorizing the call of 100 militia to each of these places on the removal of the volunteers in case the measure should then be warranted by the probability of an attack.[35]

On May 3, Porter made a similar plea to the Secretary of War for additional forces to protect the depots along the coast.

> We have probably 1000 volunteers or upwards now engaged, and if we had means we could recruit more rapidly than heretofore. I have stationed about 200, (recruited in that vicinity,) at the mouth of the Genesee River, and supplied them with arms for the protection of the public provisions deposited there.[36]

Meanwhile, Chauncey was busy tracking the British fleet.

> I have not heard from Oswego since I wrote last. The enemy's fleet left Kingston again yesterday. The Lady of the Lake dogged them until evening and was several times chased by one of their brigs. The enemy had with him a number of small vessels and gunboats and at sundown were

---

[34] Deposition of Constant Bacon, April 2, 1814, Documents, 1814:1, p. 10.

[35] General Porter to Governor Thompkins, April 8, 1814, Documents, 1814:1, p 386.

[36] General Porter to the Secretary of War, May 3, 1814, Documents, 1814:1, p. 391.

standing about S.W., evidently bound again to Oswego or the Genesee river on some marauding expedition.[37]

Chauncey was right. On May 14, 1814, the British attempted a landing at the Genesee. The defense of the small town of Charlotte, and consequently the surrounding area, was well depicted by Hanford, describing both the heroic and almost comedic actions of the army and the militia. General Porter described it as "outbullying" but in the same letter, displays his frustration at the inability to provide for any significant defense in the area.

I returned yesterday with Major Noon from the mouth of the Genesee River, where we were called on Friday last by information of the approach of the British fleet. The enclosed newspaper account is a tolerably correct relation of what took place.

We saved the town and our own credit by fairly outbullying John Bull. The discovery that we had troops, without knowing their numbers, concealed in a ravine near the mouth of the river to cut off their retreat in case they entered it, together with the tone of defiance with which we answered their demands, (the last answer having been conveyed by our friend Major Noon,) made them think it prudent to be off. We had, however, some excellent officers and good men well prepared, and in case the enemy had landed I had no doubt of a result creditable to the State.

When the enemy left Genesee they stood to the eastward, and a cannonading has been heard in the direction of Pultneyville, whither I believe General Swift had proceeded with some volunteers and militia. There is a report in town to-day that they landed at that place and took about 75 or 100 barrels of public provisions. The Oswego paper is undoubtedly genuine.

On the subject of the volunteer corps, I am still without a line from you or the Secretary of War. The silence on the part of Your Excellency is the more inexplicable, as I am sure that you can entertain no unfriendly views towards me personally. I have a. considerable body of men engaged, by

---

[37] Commodore Chauncey to the Secretary of the Navy, May 12, 1814, Documents, 1813:5, p. 347.

whom I am continually harassed by calls for contingencies, instructions, &c., &c., which it is not in my power to meet. I have neither money nor reputation to waste in pursuing the course to which a continuation of the present extraordinary state of this business must lead. But I find still greater difficulties in going back than forward. Having raised the men by your advice, I do not feel authorized to dismiss them without the same authority. I am sure I must receive something from Your Excellency shortly.[38]

Edwin Scrantom provided this account in his "Old Citizen Letters":

> On the 14th of May [1814] the British fleet, with five large and eight smaller vessels of war, appeared off the mouth of the Genesee river. The alarm being given, all the male inhabitants of the village capable of bearing arms, amounting to thirty-three, turned out with the militia of the towns around us, to prevent Sir James Yeo from landing, leaving only two men here to guard the women and children, and in case of his landing…these men were to send the families to the woods for safety, on the east side of the river. This menace was the most serious of the perplexing "scares" that agitated the village, and lasted several days….Before the little band of men left the village for Charlotte they threw up a breastwork at Deep Hollow [Lake Avenue between Glenwood and Lexington Avenues]…which was then what its name indicates, and the design of this breastwork was to shield the men from the fire of the advancing enemy, while they poured in upon them, should they attempt to cross the bridge….But the breastwork never had a sortie to give it a history, or a baptism of blood….After a parley with our men at Charlotte the fleet left, and not many days after the army of American stragglers followed suite.[39]

The British moved on from the Genesee and headed east toward the small town of Pultneyville.

> I have the honor to communicate to you an affair which took place at Pultneyville on Sunday last, between the enemy and a party of Americans consisting of 100 militia of Major

---

[38] General Porter to Governor Tompkins. May 17, 1814, <u>Documents</u>, 1814:1, p. 394.

[39] Harriet Julia Naylor, ed., "And This War Rochester! Excerpts from the Old Citizen Letters of Edwin Scranton," <u>Rochester History</u>, Volume IV (January 1942), No.1, p. 7.

Rodgers' battalion and 24 N. Y. S. Volunteers. On Thursday last I received information by express that the enemy were off Pultneyville. On Friday I was informed that the enemy still continued off that place, and had got their barges out for the purpose of landing, but a thick fog coming on deterred them from their intended project. On Saturday about 4 o'clock p. m. I received intelligence that the enemy were off that place, and had taken four prisoners from the Four-Mile Creek. I immediately ordered what volunteers I had at this place to march immediately, and used my utmost endeavors to rally the militia. I arrived at Pultneyville on Sunday at 10 o'clock a. m. The fog still continued on the lake so that it was impossible to discover anything further than a mile from the shore. At about 12 a. m. the fog cleared and the enemy's fleet to the number of four ships, one brig and one schooner, appeared about four miles distant from the shore. I then proceeded to arrange my force in the best manner I could for the purpose of being prepared in case they should attack us. At 4 p. m. the enemy sent a flag ashore and demanded the public property, and if it was not given up the village should be destroyed. My reply was that the property which remained in the storehouse at Pultneyville was property of private citizens of the U. S., and that the moment they attempted to land I should consider they invaded the American shore, and should defend it to the last extremity. After the enemy's flag had returned, several of the inhabitants informed me that there was only about 100 bbls. of damaged flour, and that if the village could be saved by sacrificing that, I had better do it. I now had two difficulties to struggle between. One was that if I permitted the enemy to land and take possession of private property on our own shores it would be injuring the honor and dignity of our country, and if I did riot do so, I was sensible that many of the inhabitants would be deprived of their all. Under these considerations I concluded that it was best to send a flag to the enemy with this proposal, that if they would land and take nothing but what property remained in the storehouse and not molest private property or individuals, they could do it. Soon after I had despatched our flag and before it had reached the enemy, I observed them to be hoisting out their boats and filling them with men. I then again proceeded immediately to arrange my force for action. A number of the enemy's boats had landed and commenced loading the flout , into their boats. A company of regulars had marched into the village and had begun to take possession of that before I had received an answer to the proposal which I had sent to the enemy. I immediately took the command of the volunteers and ordered them to commence firing, which they did in such a destructive manner that the enemy were obliged to take shelter in one of the houses to cover themselves from our fire. A number of the gunboats lay within a quarter of a mile of shore and the shipping one or two miles out. A cannonading soon commenced from them, which obliged us to retire into the woods. However, the enemy did not remain long on shore and left it so precipitately they cut their boats loose and lost several barrels of flour. I am happy to inform you that no loss was sustained on our part except the loss of about 130 barrels of musty flour. The officer that commanded the expedition on shore, it is said, was wounded, and we have reason to judge from circumstances at that time that there; must have been undoubtedly a number more wounded. The prisoners they took at the Four Mile Creek they put on shore in the first flag, but took two more when they retreated.

The public property to the amount of about 230 barrels of flour remain about three-quarters of a mile back from Putneyville.[40]

The visit was covered extensively by the press: "On Saturday, (May 14,) the enemy appeared off the villiage of Pultneyville and sent a barge ashore, which took off as prisoners a Mr. Fuller and two other persons."[41]

As the war ended, life around the lake gradually returned to normal. The residents of the southern Lake Ontario shore did not quickly forget the raids and deadly depredations caused by the British, or by the minor inconveniences caused by American troops defending the area. Erastus Spalding submitted a claim to Congress "praying compensation for damages sustained by his property, lying at the mouth of Genesee river...occasioned by its being occupied by a detachment of troops in the service of the United States."[42] Another claim, from a group of merchants at Sodus, was submitted directly to Commodore

---

[40] Brigadier-General John Swift to General Porter, May 19, 1814

[41] Newspaper? , Documents, 1813:5, p. 347.

[42] Journal of the House of Representatives of the United States, Volume 9, 13th Congress, 3rd Session, December 27, 1814. Washington, DC: Gales & Seaton, Printers, 1826, p. 618.

Yeo. Yeo's reply reiterates much of the incident in question and does well to avoid the issue of compensation.

> I have received your letter of the 25th of February, stating that in the spring of 1813 you had 200 barrels of flour in the store of Nathaniel Merrill, at Sodus Bay, on Lake Ontario, for the purpose of transporting the same to the village of Ogdensburg, for the use of the inhabitants of that vicinity, but when Sodus Bay was captured in the month of June last by the fleet under my command, the said 200 barrels were taken on board, and requesting I would cause you to be compensated for the loss you have thus sustained.
>
> In return to which I beg leave to observe, that from the respectable channel through which it was forwarded to me, I have no doubt your statement may be correct.
>
> I regret it does not come within my power to comply with your request, from the length of time which has elapsed and the sale and distribution of the property.
>
> I have, therefore, only to recommend you, gentlemen, to lay the case before such Commissioner or Board as may hereafter be appointed by our respective Governments to investigate similar claims.[43]

The incidents at Charlotte, Pultneyville, and Sodus occupy but a minor footnote in the history of the War of 1812. They are, however, an important part of the local history of the area and demonstrate the resolve and determination of the early settlers in this region.

---

[43] Reply of Commodore Yeo, March 6, 1815 in J. Ross Robertson, Robertson's Landmarks of Toronto, Toronto: J. Ross Robertson, 1896, p. 240.

# A Short Biography of Franklin Hanford

Franklins Hanford's interest in the military activities near the Genesee River originated in his upbringing in the outskirts of Rochester, New York. Born on November 8, 1844 in Chili, New York, to William Haynes Hanford and Abbey Pixley Hanford, he attended the Union School at Scottsville, New York, and Rochester High School at Rochester, New York. He entered the United States Naval Academy on November 29, 1862 but was abruptly dismissed two weeks later when it was discovered that at eighteen, he exceeded the upper age limit for admission (a recent change reducing the age from eighteen to seventeen). Hanford sought reinstatement through his Congressman, Alfred Ely. Finding the Secretary of the Navy uncooperative, Ely took Hanford to the White House, where they met with President Lincoln who ordered Hanford reinstated. The meeting with Lincoln was viewed by Hanford among his most memorable experiences which he recounted in *How I Entered the Navy: Including a Personal Interview with Abraham Lincoln.*

Hanford graduated from the Naval Academy in June 1866 and was assigned to the U.S.S. *Saco* cruising in the West Indies and Gulf of Mexico. In January 1868, he was assigned to the ship *Kearsarge* making a cruise to the South Pacific Station and was promoted to Ensign. In September 1868, Hanford was transferred to U.S.S. *Tuscarora* where he was promoted to Master in 1869 and finally to Lieutenant in 1870. In 1871, he was assigned to the flagship of the European Station, U.S.S. *Wabash*. After three years in Europe, Hanford proceeded to Newport, Rhode Island on torpedo duty and then on to New York in 1875 for service on the receiving ship *Vermont*. He served on the Asiatic Station flagship U.S.S. Tennessee and eventually returned to New York for ordnance duty at the New York Navy Yard. From 1881 to 1884, Hanford served as navigator aboard the U.S.S. *Pensacola*. In 1885, he was promoted to Lieutenant Commander and served various positions including ordnance duty at the Washington Navy Yard from 1886-1888, the Inspector of Ordnance at the West Point Foundry in Cold Springs, New York and the back to the *Pensacola* as Executive Officer. Duty here included a scientific expedition to West Africa from 1889-1890 and visiting Chili at the opening of the Rebellion of 1891. While serving as senior aid to the commandant of the New York Navy Yard from 1892 to 1895, he was promoted to Commander. His next assignment was to serve as commandant of the U.S.S. *Alert* on the Pacific Station from 1895 to 1897. Afterwards, he held the post of lighthouse inspector on the Great Lakes until 1900. Hanford was enroute to Guam on the USS

*Solace* to assume command of the USS *Yosemite*, an auxiliary cruiser station at Guam, when a typhoon damage *Yosemite* and caused her crew to scuttle the ship.[44] He assumed the office of commandant of the U.S. Naval Station at Cavite, Philippine Islands. He returned home in 1902, and retired with the rank of Rear Admiral in 1903 after 40 years of service in the Navy which included almost 21 years of sea duty on ships.[45]

Admiral Hanford retired at his home, "The Farm," at Scottsville, New York where he pursued his hobbies of collecting rare books and studying local history. He published several papers for the Scottsville Literary Society and gave speeches on historical topics before a variety of organizations. He suffered a stroke in 1912 which left him partially impaired, but continued many of his activities until his eyesight failed. Admiral Hanford died on February 8, 1928, and was buried in Oatka Cemetery at Scottsville. Hanford was married to Sarah Adelia Crosby on November 6, 1878, and had three children, Mary Crosby Hanford (1880 - 1881), John Munn Hanford (1882 - 1973), and Ruth Crosby Hanford (1887 - 1976). His papers, correspondence, and historical writings are part of the historical collections at the Rush Rhees Library at the University of Rochester.[46]

---

[44] *New York Times*, November 29, 1900.

[45] Register of Commissioned and Warrant Officers of the United States Navy and Marine Corps, January 1, 1917, Washington, DC: Government Prining Office, 1917.

[46] Admiral Hanford's biographical information was obtained from Lewis Randolph Hamersly, The Records of Living Officers of the U.S. Navy and Marine Corps Compiled from Official Sources, Seventh Edition, New York: L.R. Hamersly Co., 1902, p 120-21, and the University of Rochester description of the Hanford Collection at the Rush Rhees Library.

# Illustrations

Cover - Map of State of New York by William McCalpin, Cartographer, 1808, New York Public Library, Digital Image ID: 434761.

Page 6 - Melancthon Taylor Woolsey - U.S. Naval Historical Center, image NH-42080.

Page 7 - Plan of the *Oneida*. From www.modelismonaval.com/magazine/oneida/historia.html.

Page 9 - Commodore Chauncey – painting by Gilbert Stuart (1775-1828) in the U.S. Naval Academy Museum Collection. U.S. Naval Historical Center, image KN-10889.

Page 13 - The Old Hanford Tavern, Rochester, NY, Photographed by James M. Angle, 1883 Albert R. Stone Negative Collection, Rochester Museum & Science Center, www.rochester.lib.ny.us.

Page 15 - Drawing of the engagement on August 10, 1813 - Color-tinted drawing by Masters Mate Peter W. Spicer, who served on board USS *Oneida* during this action. U.S. Naval Historical Center, image NH 75733-KN.

Page 17 - Drawing of the engagement on September 11, 1813 - Color-tinted drawing by Masters Mate Peter W. Spicer, who served on board USS *Sylph* during this action. U.S. Naval Historical Center, image NH 75734-KN.

Page 18 - Sir James Yeo - Metropolitan Toronto Reference Library, J. Ross Robertson Collection, T15241.

Page 20 - Drawing of schooner *Growler* captured by the British. Artist unknown.

Page 26 - Drawing of engagement between Naval engagement off the Genesee River, Sir James Yeo on HMS *Wolfe* vs. Commodore Chauncey on USS *General Pike*, September 11, 1813, from CH. J. Snider, In the Wake of the Eighteen-Twelvers, p. 48.

Page 28 – Possible ruins of Ft. Bender. Albert R. Stone Negative Collection, Rochester Museum & Science Center, www.rochester.lib.ny.us.

Page 30 - Early Rochester map showing the bridge over the Genesee River, Central Library of Rochester and Monroe County, www.vintageviews.org.

Page 32 - Elisha Ely – photo from Marcia Ihrig Fotopoulos on hometownvalue.com website.

Page 35 - Bridge over the Genesee River – Central Library of Rochester and Monroe County, www.vintageviews.org.

Page 38 - Peter B. Porter in Benson Lossing's Pictorial Fieldbook of the War of 1812, page 838.

Page 39 - General Izard in Benson Lossing's Pictorial Fieldbook of the War of 1812, page 845.

Page 41 – USS *Scourge*, formerly *Lord Nelson*. The Hamilton-Scourge Project, www.hamilton-scourge.hamilton.ca/the-schooners.asp.

Page 45 – HMS *Royal George* under chase by the Lake Ontario Squadron. Unknown artist. From canadianhistory.suite101.com.

Page 56 - Battle on Lake Ontario. From the collections of The Mariners' Museum, Newport News, VA.

# Bibliography

The works cited below include those works used by Hanford in <u>Notes on the Visits</u> as well as additional works used in producing this study which also provide excellent background information on the actions on Lake Ontario.

Abbott, Willis J. <u>Blue Jackets of 1812</u>. New York: Dodd, Mead & Company, 1897.

Cooper, James Fenimore. <u>History of the Navy of the United States of America</u>. 2 vols. Philadelphia: Thomas, Cowpertwait & Co., 1847.

Cooper, James Fenimore. <u>Lives of Distinguished Naval Officers</u>. Philadelphia: Carey & Hart, 1846.

Cruikshank, Ernest A., ed. <u>The Documentary History of the Campaign upon the Niagara Frontier in the Year 1812, 1813, 1814</u>. 4 vols., Reprint Edition: Arno Press Inc., 1971.

Dudley, William J., and Crawford, Michael J., eds. <u>The Naval War of 1812: A Documentary History</u>, 3 vols., Washington, DC: Naval Historical Center, 1985, 1992, 2002.

Fay, Heman Allen. <u>Collection of the Official Accounts, in Detail, of all the Battles fought by Sea and Land, between the United States, and the Navy and Army of Great Britain, During the years 1812, 13, 14 & 15</u>. New York: E. Conrad, 1817.

James, William. <u>Full and Correct Account of the Chief Naval Occurances of the Late War Between Great Britain and the United States of America</u>. London: T. Egerton, 1817.

James, William. <u>Naval History of Great Britain</u>. Vol. 6. London: Richard Bentley, 1837.

Lossing, Benson J. <u>Pictorial Fieldbook of the War of 1812</u>. New York: Harper & Brothers, 1869.

Mahan, Alfred Thayer. <u>Sea Power in its Relation to the War of 1812</u>. 2 vols. Boston: Little, Brown & Co., 1905.

Malcomson, Robert. <u>Lords of the Lake</u>. Toronto: R. Bass Studio, 1998.

Malcomson, Robert, ed., <u>Sailors of 1812: Memoirs and letters of Naval Officers on Lake Ontario</u>, Youngstown, NY: Old Fort Niagara Association, 1997.

Marsh, Ruth and Truesdale, Dorothy S., "War on Lake Ontario: 1812-1815," <u>Rochester History</u>, vol. IV (October, 1942), no. 4.

Naylor, Harriett Julia, ed., "And This Was Rochester! Excerpts from the Old Citizen Letters of Edwin Scrantom," Rochester History, vol. IV (January 1942), no. 1.

O'Reilly, Henry. Sketches of Rochester. Rochester, NY: W. Alling, 1838.

Robertson, J. Ross. Robertson's Landmarks of Toronto, Toronto: J. Ross Robertson, 1896.

Roemer, Lillian, "The Genesee River During the War of 1812, " Rochester History, vol. LIII (Fall, 1991), no. 4.

Roosevelt, Theodore. Naval War of 1812. 2 vols. New York: Putnam, 1897.

Turner, O., History of the Pioneer Settlement of Phelp's and Gorham's Purchase and Morris' Reserve, Rochester, NY: William Alling, 1851.

Printed in Great Britain
by Amazon.co.uk, Ltd.,
Marston Gate.